Contents

Clay stream
from a Cornish
china clay pit

The New
Potter's Companion

The New Potter's Companion

Tony Birks

Collins

The picture on page 1 shows composite pots by Hans Coper.

Designed and produced by Alphabet and Image Ltd, Sherborne, Dorset
First published as *The Potter's Companion* 1974
Revised edition published 1982 by
William Collins Sons and Co Ltd,
Glasgow and London
ISBN 0 00 411856 1

The extracts from *A Potter's Book* by Bernard Leach
are reproduced by kind permission of Faber and Faber Ltd,
London, and Transatlantic Arts Inc., New York.

Printed and bound in England by Robert Hartnoll Ltd, Bodmin, Cornwall.

1 Earth, fire and water

The earth yields up pottery in a surprising way. Not only does every garden spade reveal an assortment of blue and white glazed fragments, but the earth itself is the very essence of pottery, and if undisturbed, pot fragments and clayey earth will lie together, unchanged, for centuries.

The pottery fragment *may* be worth looking at—for it can have a story to tell. I recently picked up a dull fawn-coloured fragment which was the bottom of a hand-thrown pot, un-glazed, with the marks underneath of the thread which had cut it from the wheel and on the side a finger mark made by the potter. The spot was a well known Roman site, and the piece, like many more from the same area, came from the hands of a potter nearly 2,000 years ago. With pottery going back as far as civilisation itself, there is nothing remarkable about such a find—the pot was not complete, after all— and since pottery does not decay like iron or wood, pottery sherds are often as common as weeds on an archaeological site. But the potter's fingerprints, and the evidence of a continuing and timeless technique made the experience a moving one. It was the bottom of a vessel for liquid; probably a jug. It was made on the wheel, from local clay, just as it could have been made today.

Techniques have been refined, of course, and the ceramics industry is a highly precise one, but the basic principles have not changed. Nor has the attraction of pottery-making lessened as it has become more mechanised, for clay, raw in its natural state or fired as a finished pot, has a strong tactile appeal, and making pottery can be an exhilarating experience.

This book is intended to be a practical guide and companion to the many people who, for whatever reason, want to become involved with pottery at the making stage. It is an immense field and many who take up pottery as a craft are rather hazy about both the essential materials and essential processes. Instructions begin in Chapter 2 and these are intended to be as full as possible for the beginner. The more experienced potter will find the later chapters deal with more advanced matters, and he can turn directly to what interests him. Meanwhile, this chapter must help the beginner with a few definitions.

Clay shows every mark: the lines of the thread used to cut the pot from the wheel; the fingerprints of the Roman potter who made it.

Pottery is made from a common, naturally occurring material, subjected to intense heat in a furnace. Clay does not become pottery until all the water it contains both in a free and a chemically combined form has been removed by heat, and when this is done, by firing in a kiln, the hard permanent result is in a stable state, and is more permanent than many kinds of rock. It can, of course, be broken up into pieces, but it is hard to get rid of the pieces. They will not dissolve or melt, or combine with other chemicals, and if they are covered with a surface of glass or glaze, they are even more impregnable.

Clay is weathered, decomposed granite and consists mainly of alumina and silica. Where clay lies in deep beds near its origin it is likely to be fairly pure, as in the case of the china clay deposits of Cornwall which surround the granite outcrop of Bodmin Moor. The clay makes the streams run white, and the waste-heaps where it is mined are ghostly like the mountains on the moon. The china clay or *kaolin* is the real mother clay—only silica, alumina and water. All its descendants contain impurities and, funnily enough, it is the impurities which give clays their character and value for the studio potter. The further the alumina-silica is carried by rainwater and the leaching effects of rain and gravity from its source rock, the more likely it is to pick up other elements. Ball clay from Newton Abbot, near Dartmoor, is almost as pure as china clay, but clay which occurs widely as a deposited material (i.e. transported and sedimented under water), especially in geologically recent areas, contains grains of silica as sand. Revealed in road cuttings and often turned up in the garden, it is yellow or blue-grey with the elements—notably iron—which have leached into it and become diffused. The coarse brick clays of the English Midlands show their iron content in the rusty pink colour they turn after they have been burnt or fired in the kiln, and many other elements—calcium, titanium, sodium and potassium—occur in small but significant proportions. The potter does not need to be a chemist to discover that the more 'impure' the clay, the better working quality it may have. This does not mean that a pot can be thrown on the wheel from clay containing roots, rotting leaves and shells, yet once the organic matter has been sieved out, the home clay-digger may have to put in his own additives such as fine sand to make the clay 'plastic' or malleable again. It is very tempting to use clay which one has dug out of the ground with one's own spade, but it is extremely tiring. At the end of the day it will still require a great deal of energy before it can be used. The clay needs 'conditioning' by a long period (years) of exposure to the weather, and the sieving and homogenisation of the clay is a slow and laborious business. It has to be tested for its working qualities, its brittleness and its shrinkage. Once prepared and made plastic by additives, the home-dug clay can still disappoint by losing its unusual colour in the kiln, and possibly by exploding or cracking under the strain of high temperatures.

The studio potter benefits by using clay which is carefully

Two identical pots, one (left) freshly made, the other biscuit and glaze fired. The shrinkage is 12 per cent and the pots now look very different.

prepared for industrial use—often a blend of materials from several sources—and if he is interested in its chemistry, an analysis will be readily provided by the suppliers. The raw material is usually called 'the body', and this body is 'clothed' with glass, though in pots like porous plant-pots the body goes naked.

The sequence of creating a pot is as follows. The shape is made by one of three methods. It is either *thrown on the wheel* (see Chapters 3–7), *made by hand* without mechanical aids (see Chapters 8 and 9) or *made with liquid or plastic clay using moulds or other industrial tools* (Chapters 10 and 11). After shaping the pot from clay in a wet or plastic form, the clay must dry out completely in the atmosphere before it is heated in the kiln. It shrinks in size as it loses this 'free' water. In the kiln it shrinks again when the chemically bound water leaves the clay at about 600° Centigrade—roughly the temperature of the element in an electric radiator or the tip of a smouldering cigarette. The temperature in the kiln is usually taken to about 1,000°C, and after cooling the pot is taken out solid, insoluble, permanent and porous. At this stage it is known as 'biscuit' ware. The experience from which it has emerged is called the 'biscuit firing'. The pot is then covered with powdered glass, and re-fired in the kiln so that the powder covering melts and resolidifies on the surface as a glaze. The result is no longer porous, and the glazed pot is ready for use. This second firing is called the glaze or glost firing.

The two firings often take place one after the other in the same kiln, and the terms 'biscuit kiln' and 'glost kiln', confusing for the beginner, simply mean *the kiln packed for a biscuit firing* and *the kiln packed for a glost firing.*

Just to complicate matters, an important method of pottery making in studio potteries is the combining of the biscuit and glost firing in a single process known as 'raw glazing' or 'once firing', in which the pot passes only once through the ordeal of high temperatures. While it is economical on fuel, it can have a high failure rate.

Decoration of the ware can take place at any stage from the making of the pot from plastic clay to a patterning of the glazed surface, and this latter practice involves a third (or second glaze) firing, though it is normally undertaken only in industrial potteries.

The terms *earthenware* and *stoneware* are familiar to many beginners, and describe the two main kinds of pottery, the result of firing to different temperatures in the second (glost) firing. Earthenware is fired to between 1,000°C and 1,100°C, enough to melt the glaze but not high enough to change the character of the body inside. At around 1,150°C the clay itself begins to vitrify, or to become fused together as a solid non-porous mass, and when vitrification has taken place the pot becomes stoneware. Most stoneware firings are between 1,250°C and 1,300°C, because it is at this temperature that the glaze takes on its best character. At all temperatures between 650°C and 1,500°C it is possible to make pottery with satisfactory glazes, but most wares made industrially and

in studios cluster in the two temperature zones 1,000°–1,100°C and 1,250°C–1,300°C as these yield the most satisfactory results. In each case the clay body, the glaze and the kiln must be suited to the temperature. Glazes are formulated to 'mature' at precise temperatures, and give of their best only when within 10° of this temperature. On the other hand both clays and kilns work satisfactorily at all temperatures up to a known maximum. For example, above 1,000°C a certain clay may 'bloat' or blister or even explode, and a kiln may simply cease to increase in temperature or, if electric, its elements may burn out.

Clays and kilns are often known by these maximum temperatures and called earthenware (1,100°C max.) clays or stoneware (1,300°C max.) kilns. It does not mean that they cannot successfully be used for work at lower temperatures. An earthenware bowl can be made with stoneware clay in a stoneware kiln—provided it is fired to earthenware temperatures and has an earthenware glaze. It is really a question of common sense, and can be summed up as follows. *Do not try to fire a clay or a kiln to a temperature higher than its known maximum and make sure that the glaze is right for the temperature used.* A 'hard' glaze which requires a high temperature will simply not melt if the temperature is too low, and it will run off into liquid pools (causing damage to the kiln) if the temperature is taken too high.

Earthenware is porous, not very dense or heavy and its glazes are usually shiny and bright. Stoneware is denser for the clay has fused together, and is therefore heavier than an earthenware pot of the same size; its glazes are usually duller and often mottled. A well-known branch of stoneware is porcelain, which is often translucent and light in weight. It needs a special pure clay and glaze, but is fired at stoneware temperatures.

Provided the equipment is available, the beginner can work in any branch of pottery. It is very sad that earthenware is traditionally regarded as more suitable for beginners, with the promise of stone-

ware and porcelain as some kind of nebulous goal for the future. It is true that some potteries are only equipped with earthenware kilns and earthenware 'red' clays, though stoneware clays are no dearer, but if it is practical the beginner will gain most if he works with coarse refractory stoneware clays and simple stoneware glazes, since earthenware demands more precision of handling to achieve a result of the same quality. A great many individual potters and small studios specialise in stoneware. One reason why the vast majority of industrial pottery is earthenware is that it takes less energy in the kiln to produce the finished result. An expensive number of kilowatts is used up in producing the final 150°C of heat.

Perhaps it is the precision of the industrial earthenware product, coupled with its frequently lifeless design which causes a reaction of taste linking liveliness of form with imprecision of execution. There is no need for a mass-produced pot to be lifeless and dull, and there is certainly no need for hand-made pots to be clumsy. A curious double standard causes some people to buy, with obvious satisfaction, mugs for drinking coffee and casseroles for baking in the oven of shocking clumsiness, whilst they would criticise a dining chair or an electric razor for the slightest fault. They have lost their ability to judge craftsmanship by the same high standards they now apply to machine-made precision goods.

The pottery studio is not the place for precision work, but this really need not be an excuse for a lack of grace or finish. Hastily or badly-made pots are all the more unreasonable when one bears in mind the total length of time required to complete an individual pot. To begin by insisting on the highest standards, however, is a mistake, for until one has completed a pot there is nothing by which to judge the next.

Illusions are shattered on the very first evening for the newcomer to an evening class hoping to go home loaded with coffee pots and useful dishes, and it is inevitably disappointing that the first term's work will probably consist of a few finished pots, produced near the term's end. Most beginners find progress tediously slow and classes frustrating. Learning pottery, for some reason, is not a steady and progressive climb, but a series of jumps, with the occasional backward slide. When one has just made a jump—a major step of progress—and suddenly a whole host of pots from one's own hands appear as if by magic, the frustrations and disappointments are all forgotten, and there is a real sense of exhilaration, which is a joy both to teacher and pupil alike.

2 Preparing the clay

Like milk, clay is usually seen first not in its natural form, but ready packaged and treated for use. Chapter 1 described its origins, but most beginners first encounter pottery clay fresh from a polythene bag. Polythene, when intact and sealed, is airtight, and clay can be kept for many years in this way. As soon as the bag is punctured or the top left untied, however, it will begin to lose moisture and harden. Loss of moisture does not cause damage but the clay has to be softened up again before use and this takes time. It can of course be bought in powder form (this is the more normal practice in the United States) which reduces transport costs but adds considerably to the labour of preparation. Nearly 30 per cent of the clay in a plastic or malleable state is water, so a ton of powdered clay is more valuable to the professional potter than its plastic equivalent, but most beginners are not concerned with this sort of quantity, and will use new plastic clay straight from the bag, or secondhand clay from the bin, where it is in the process of re-cycling.

Quite a lot of clay never gets as far as the kiln, having suffered some accident in the making process, and this 'used' clay is often more responsive the second time round, so the beginner need not feel he is having to work with faulty materials. In any case, new or old, his clay will need preparing for use.

Making the clay ready is sometimes hard work, and is too often skimped; inadequately prepared clay will usually fail during the making of a pot or at a later stage and in either case it is maddening. Plastic clay for pots must be prepared in the same way whichever technique is to be used. The object of this preparation is to ensure that the clay has a perfectly even texture, and this is achieved by a combination of cutting the clay across with a nylon thread or a wire and re-forming it or 'wedging', and exerting pressure on it with the hands. Often described as kneading, this latter technique is the very first one the beginner will learn, and it is a slight misnomer, for dough and clay behave in different ways.

The potter takes a piece of plastic clay not smaller than the size of his two fists and places it in front of him on a clean flat surface. Potteries usually have wedging benches very solidly built so that they can support a good deal of weight, and stand firm against the sideways pressure of the hands on the clay. The best surface for the bench top is slate, which is more absorbent than marble but less so than wood or plaster. The heel or pad of muscle at the base of the palms of both hands is pressed against the clay, away from the body. As the clay is pushed away by this action, the fingertips retrieve it and pull the edge of the clay over and back into position so that pressure can be applied again by the heel of the hand. Thus a rhythmic and circular motion is set up which is continuous.

The clay should not stick to the flat surface. If it does, it is either too wet (and should be replaced by a drier piece or dried with additives—see page 15) or the potter is acting too quickly on it and should attempt a more rhythmic movement. If the piece of clay becomes too long and sausage-like by this process, the sausage should be stood on its end, pressed down into a more compact lump, and the process re-begun. This regular reorganisation of the clay helps to give it an even texture. Some beginners find the clay becoming 'greasy', and this is because they are stroking it and not

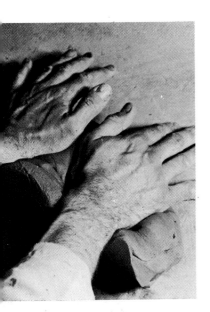

The hands press the clay forwards and the fingertips retrieve it in a continuous folding process called kneading.

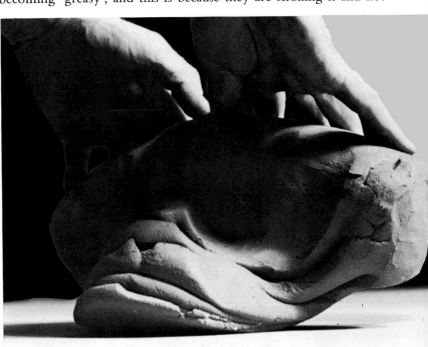

Left: by applying more downward pressure with the heel of one hand or the other the clay will be kneaded into a compact spiral like an ammonite.

using enough force; they should use the heel of the hand more and the fingertips less. Some manage to produce a combination of greasiness and cracking, and the reason here is usually that they have cosmetics on the hands. Clay does make some people's skin dry; it is best to let this happen whilst potting and use a moisturising cream afterwards. A piece of clay which has become cracked on the surface is not fit for use and should be put back in the bin for re-conditioning.

The classic shape of clay in preparation is shown in the picture on page 13 and the technique is often learned in minutes. When this has been completely mastered it can be varied if desired into a spiral form. By putting more pressure with the heel of the right or left hand, a spiral shape will quickly emerge and if this can be controlled an even texture is most rapidly achieved. Clay which is kneaded spirally remains a constant shape throughout, shown above, which adds to the potter's convenience. It is not necessary to learn the spiral technique, but it is this method which is usually adopted by experienced potters who want to prepare a lot of clay quickly.

A length of twisted copper wire, with a bobbin attached to each end, or a similar length of nylon thread as used by fishermen is the tool used to cut through the kneaded clay, like wire through cheese, to investigate the state of the inside. If the wire is passed through the lump of clay at several levels, the slices can be peeled off and the cross-section examined. Evening-class clay commonly includes pieces of sponge, lumps of Plaster of Paris, metal screws, hairs (very destructive to pots on the wheel) and other foreign bodies which must be rooted out. If the average-sized lump of clay is cut through at half-inch intervals, the slices separated and reassembled, and cut through again at right angles to the first cuts, it is likely that these hidden objects will come to light. So will cracks, air pockets and

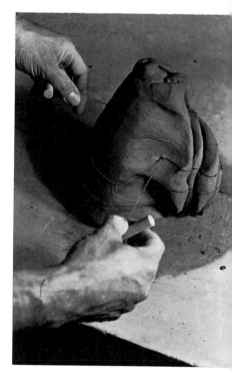

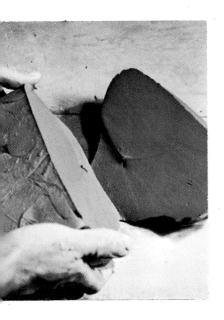

any hard lumps. A single slice, thrown down on the wedging table, will spread out on impact and any weakness in the clay will show up as a crack or cavity. The cure for all such faults is simply to continue wedging and kneading the clay, and to slice up the lump at intervals until all the faults have disappeared. It is sensible, when reassembling slices to re-form the lump, to turn each slice over before joining it to its neighbour, so that the clay within the lump will be very thoroughly mixed. For the serious student, the exercise of mixing two different-coloured clays in slices, like a multi-decker sandwich, and then kneading them together, will clearly illustrate how the technique shown in the picture sequence circulates the clay within the lump until it is all perfectly mixed. If the kneading process is done correctly air pockets are not trapped in the clay by the continuous folding. Beginners often fail to see any improvement in the quality of the clay they are preparing, and the reason may be that they are trying to tackle too large a lump of clay. Halving the quantity is often the answer.

Certain additives can improve the working qualities of the clay, or improve its texture or appearance. Most common of these is grog, which is quite simply ground-down pottery which has been fired in the kiln. This can be as fine as flour or as coarse as granulated sugar, and because it is absorbent it has the immediate effect of drying the clay. It is worked into the clay at the wedging stage, like fine currants into a pudding. Grog usually helps to give the clay a longer working life on the wheel. The pot will stay up longer without collapsing, and coarse grog (or silver sand) gives an attractive texture to the finished pot, although some beginners may find it distractingly scratchy to the hands. Colouring stains can be added to the clay at the wedging stage in the form of metal oxides or

Carry on kneading until the clay is quite smooth. You can check this by cutting the clay into slices with a wire (left and right): air bubbles, hard lumps or extraneous matter will show where the clay is cut through (above).

carbonates—small quantities are sufficient to affect the colour of the clay when fired—and the colours are described in Chapter 12. Oxides are mainly black before firing and some potteries choose *not* to wedge the colourant too evenly into the clay, preferring the random appearance of coloured spots and patches when the clay is fired.

The potter will soon find the optimum working hardness for clay for use on the wheel, and that clay which is too hard or too soft can add to his difficulties. To test for hardness, try pressing your thumb against it. The clay should yield readily, but should not stick to your thumb when you take it away. If the potter is working on the wheel he will divide his lump of prepared clay into several balls. Clay loses moisture quickly and if put on to an absorbent wooden surface the underside of the ball will become dry and hard, so it is sensible to pile the balls together like cannon balls on a sheet of polythene which can be wrapped around them if necessary.

Once prepared for the wheel, clay can be stored wrapped in polythene for a very long time. As wedging and kneading can be quite exhausting, many potters sensibly prefer to exhaust themselves first, and take a rest before throwing on the wheel. The beginner who does not need to prepare such tiringly large quantities should aim to have at least half a dozen pieces of clay ready to use, even if he has only a few minutes on the wheel. The life of a piece of clay, when one is learning to throw, may be only a few seconds, and it is frustrating and disruptive to have to leave the wheel to prepare more clay in mid-stream.

Equally, hand-made pots not made on the wheel are best made from a single batch of clay, and if such a pot is not finished in one session, it is important to wrap and store enough clay for later use so that you can complete the job.

3 Starting work on the wheel

The traditional wheel is characterised by its large flywheel.

The magic of turning a solid ball of clay into a perfect symmetrical pot in a matter of seconds draws most beginners to the wheel. It is not necessarily the technique which makes the 'best' pots but it is the best way to learn to handle clay.

Beginners, forced through lack of wheel facilities to start with hand-made pots can turn directly to Chapter 8 for guidance, though my advice to them is to acquaint themselves with the wheel and wheel techniques as early as possible. This chapter, together with the next four, takes the beginner through the various stages.

Wheels

A great deal of strong emotion surrounds the question of choice of pottery wheels. Essentially, a wheel is a smoothly revolving platform capable of variable speeds of rotation, and generally turning a good deal slower than the beginner imagines. Power to turn the wheel can be supplied by the potter, using his feet on a pedal or flywheel, or by some other form like electricity. For the beginner it is best to start on a good electric wheel. Pedalling, like riding a bicycle, usually shakes the body a bit and one needs to be distracted as little as possible from the business of controlling what one's hands are doing. Many potters prefer to work on a foot-controlled wheel, but usually only after they have learned to judge their 'power requirements' in advance, and to use the heavy flywheel to advantage.

The greatest and most common defects of wheels are worn bearings, making the wheel-head shudder and wobble, and a jerky 'clutch', which starts and stops the wheel violently. Both faults are trying to the best of potters and if the beginner has any choice at all, he should avoid a wheel with these bad habits.

Centering

The first act in making a pot on a wheel is to centre the clay. There is no one way of centering, though one thing is quite certain: it is not possible to throw a perfect pot from a piece of clay which is not

Put the clay on a dry wheel-head with dry hands. Then wet your hands and the clay so that they will not stick to each other.

running true. It is essential to master a technique for centering at the outset. A student who can cope with some of the later stages of shaping and finishing the pot, but who cannot centre the clay without help from the teacher is in a pathetic position; left to his own devices he can do nothing at all.

Probably the difficulty of centering clay accounts for more despair and disillusionment amongst beginners than anything else. This is because centering is a knack; once you have the knack it is not only easy but, when the clay is running true at all speeds and responding to the pressure of your hands, a positive pleasure. When you have reached this stage, you can congratulate yourself.

The centrifugal force of the revolving wheel will try to fling an uneven piece of clay off the wheel-head altogether, and the faster the wheel is turning, the harder it will try. Only when the weight of the clay is so perfectly balanced in the centre of the wheel that the centrifugal forces are equal on all sides will the clay revolve evenly, docile and obedient.

One might as well minimise the difficulties by making the lump of clay as round as possible before starting, and ensuring that the piece chosen is properly wedged, and not too hard. The amount of clay a beginner can control will depend on the size of his hands, but as a general guide a piece weighing about 1 lb or 500 grams, or about the size of a large orange—rather larger than a tennis ball—would not be out of the way.

Do *not* throw the ball of clay on to a spinning wheel. You are almost certain to miss the centre of the wheel, even at close range, and there is a good chance that you will miss the wheel-head altogether and it will land in the waterbowl or on the floor. Start with the wheel stationary, and place the clay carefully in the centre of a dry wheel-head, pressing firmly against the surface without distorting the shape.

Make sure that your hands as well as the wheel-head are dry before taking this first step. A layer of water underneath the clay will prevent it from sticking, for water acts on clay as a lubricant like oil. Though water will eventually soften and break down the structure of plastic clay, a film of water is needed on your hands to prevent them sticking to the clay when developing the pot on the wheel. If too little water is used, the clay will become stubborn and obtuse. Paradoxically, the more water, the less sticky the clay, though a wheel swimming with water should be avoided as it makes working conditions difficult and soaks one's clothes.

As soon as the wheel is set in motion, the unevenness of the clay will be apparent. Centering can now begin; no tools are needed, just hands lubricated with water. If you hold your hands loosely over the clay they will wobble as the uneven ball goes round. If you were able to hold your hands absolutely rigid like a steel template, the clay would automatically centre itself underneath them, but it is quite difficult to hold your hands still as the wheel revolves, and the wobbles are apt to get worse and worse. Whether

you are sitting or standing at the wheel, make sure that your elbows are firmly braced against the wheel surround—there is usually a rubber padding here for comfort. Encompass the whole of the clay using both hands, either locked together at the fingertips with the thumbs covering the centre, or with the left hand at the side of the ball and the right hand over the top.

The wheel should be rotating quite fast; trying to centre a piece of clay with the wheel turning slowly adds to one's problems, and an experienced potter will centre the clay in a second or two, with the wheel turning faster than at any later stage. A beginner using a kick-wheel should get up a good deal of speed before putting his hands to the clay, so that he does not have to concentrate on speeding the wheel while his mind is on other things.

Pressure exerted on the clay inwards from the side will raise the clay up in a cone; pressure from above will lower it again, and this movement helps to remove the wobbles. The hands should not be separated but pressure applied alternately, first from the side and then from above so that the clay can change shape underneath them. If you clasp both hands around the clay and draw them with increasing pressure towards your body, the clay will rise rapidly upwards in a cone—it is taking the line of least resistance. Pressure evenly applied from the thumbs will reduce the cone to a low dome. By raising and lowering the clay several times by one of these

Press with your left hand to raise the clay, your right one to lower it.

methods, the clay will be encouraged into being 'on centre'. When the hands can be kept perfectly still while the clay revolves beneath them the job is done. Beginners who find the experience of centering maddeningly difficult *must* persevere until they get the knack. A state of war with the revolving clay often ends in victory for the clay, but can be avoided if the potter forgets his adversary and concentrates on holding his hands still.

Beginners sometimes find that some of the clay will squeeze out between the two hands or thumbs as pressure is applied, making a mushroom shape, or if it is flattened too severely with downward pressure that a sticky, hollow 'navel' appears when pressure from the side raises the clay again. If this starts to happen, the position of the hands should be changed until the clay is comfortably contained. If air, or a pool of water, is locked into the centred clay it is bound to cause trouble when the pot is being formed, and to avoid this the clay must be kept in a compact piece.

There is no 'correct' way of holding the hands around the clay whilst centering, only the general rule that they must contain the clay, and be capable of being held quite still while the wheel turns fast.

Clasp both hands together and pull towards your chest. The clay will rise in a cone.

When the lump is centred, remove the sticky clay from the wheel-head.

4 Opening up

With the clay spinning truly on the wheel-head the potter is ready for the next stage. Starting to open up the clay into a pot provides another minor ordeal for the beginner. A hole is made down the centre of the ball with the thumb of the right hand, or with both thumbs together, and many find it hard to prevent the thumb wobbling on the way down. The hole must run as true as the clay for if the hole is off-centre within the lump, the result is exactly the same as a perfect hole in an off-centred piece of clay—more material on one side than the other.

The first aid to learning this technique is to make a hollow in the top of the clay with the index finger of the right hand; lay it on the clay and move it towards the centre, pressing slightly downwards. Take it away gently and there will be a slight hollow. Now the thumb will have something to aim at in making the hole.

Make a dimple with your forefinger in the middle of the centred clay.

The next aid is to brace the forearms on the sides of the wheel, and to lock the hands together, the left hand gripping the back of the right hand near the wrist. This should leave the right thumb free. Point it vertically downwards. Now lower it slowly into the ball of clay. Go too far and you will meet the metal surface of the wheel-head. Be too timid and the pot will have a base so thick that it will always feel elephantine, even if it does not crack in the kiln. Ideally, the hole inside should go to within $\frac{1}{2}$ inch (about 1 cm) of the wheel-head. Practice alone teaches you when you have gone far enough, though if you clear away the sticky clay from around the edge of the base of the lump at least you will see where the top of the wheel-head is.

Having made the hole do not withdraw your thumb but push it sideways away from you to widen the base of the hole. Try to keep the tip of the thumb at a constant level, so that the base is flat, and make the movement *slowly*.

Everything done on the wheel is best done slowly. Rapid movements cause spirals which are ugly and destructive, and movements which are started slowly must also be finished slowly. A sudden end to the process of widening the base will be as destructive as a sudden beginning—and the pot will wobble.

Some potters find that an airlock is caused at this stage, with their

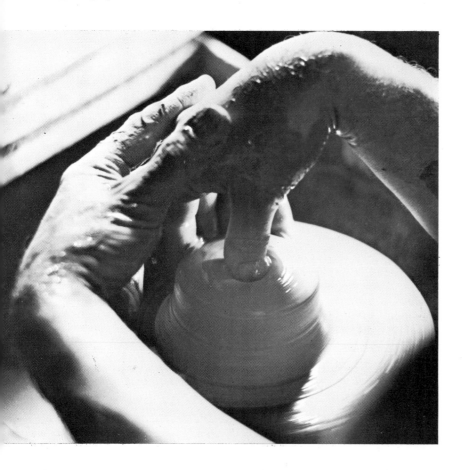

An unsupported thumb wobbles, or makes an eccentric hole as shown above. Linking hands (top left) will steady it. Left: the ink-well stage.

thumb inside the pot, and that a vacuum is being produced as they widen the base. If this is the case withdraw the thumb *slowly*, until the airlock is broken, and then replace it along with a little water. The fingers of the right hand, which have so far been left outside the clay can now be used. Let them grasp the outside of the form firmly, on the far side away from your body. Then draw the hand slowly upwards and towards you. With fingers outside and thumb inside, about ¾ inch (2 cm) apart, the clay will rise up between them and, if all is well, when the hand gently leaves the clay a hollow shape will have been made. Commonly called the 'inkwell' shape, it is probably easier to remember if likened to an upturned flowerpot. This process which takes so long to describe, and often takes hours to learn, should all be accomplished in a single movement lasting about five seconds. As one gets more experienced one should aim at producing a firm corner to the inside of the base and an even thickness of wall as in the diagram.

The action so far has come from the right hand only. The left hand is used for steadying, though some potters prefer to begin the opening-up using both hands, making the same movements exactly together. At the next stage the two hands have different functions; make sure both are thoroughly moist by dipping them in the water bowl. The *left* hand is used inside the pot and the fingertips of as many fingers (not thumb) as you can get into the pot are pressed gently against the base of the wall. The *right* hand is used *outside* the pot, and the index finger is crooked so that the flat section between the first and second knuckles can be pressed down on the wheel-head. The side of the index finger then will naturally

When drawing up the basic cylinder, lock your hands together for steadiness.

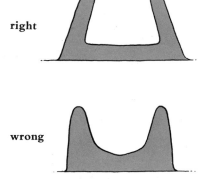

right

wrong

fit against the wall or side of the pot. Both hands can be drawn upwards together. The clay, squeezed between the left and right hand, has nowhere to go but upwards, and in a few seconds a tall cylinder is made.

I strongly advise left-handed beginners to adopt the right-handed pattern of throwing rather than reversing all the instructions, as both hands are used to an equal extent on the wheel, and electric wheels are designed to turn anticlockwise so that the potter can see the effects of his actions from the downstream side. I have never known a left-hander who has had difficulty in following the instructions given in this chapter.

The beginner is now in the very thick of it, and with so many things going on it is difficult for him to concentrate on three additional factors, but he will make great strides if he can maintain three constants: *constant speed of the wheel* (rather slower than for centering—perhaps half the speed), *a constant distance apart for the hands*, and *a constant speed of movement up the pot*. All three are factors in maintaining an even thickness in the wall of the pot. With practice, the hands will be able to withdraw slowly from the top of the clay to leave an even cylinder, running true, on the wheel. By repeating the same motion two or three times from the bottom of

When the basic cylinder is made, more pressure from inside will widen the shape. By using both hands to throttle the neck from outside you can make it narrow again.

the pot to the top, the clay wall can be narrowed to a sensible thickness and the cylinder will reach its 'natural' height.

Putting shape into the cylinder can be described and understood very simply—though putting it into practice often takes a lifetime, for the potter's aesthetic sense as well as his practical ability is now tested. Stated briefly, greater pressure from the inside will make the pot swell and the walls belly outwards, greater pressure from the outside will constrict the pot and make a neck or 'collar'. Left to its own devices the spinning cylinder, helped by centrifugal force, would eventually widen out and flatten itself like a pancake on the wheel. Thus more pressure is needed to narrow the pot from outside than to widen the pot from within, as one has to act against the centrifuge. For a really effective narrowing, both hands are used around the pot exactly as if one were throttling it, thumbs facing you, fingers round the far side. If the pot is closed up to a narrow neck, it is important to make sure that all the water has been sponged out from the bottom before it is too late to get the sponge inside.

These are the basic principles for making a pot on the wheel. Using the hands in concert, one lengthens then widens or narrows the form. One aspect of the form is fixed by the technique; the wheel ensures that the plan of the pot is circular. The profile of the outside is the potter's affair, and practice will give him expertise in correcting faults as they appear, and anticipation so that they do not happen.

The commonest fault of all beginners is to make the wall of the pot too thin near the base so that the top ring of clay twists off and stays in the hands of the potter while the base turns merrily on. The temptation at this point is to alter one's intention from making a vase to making an ashtray. Do resist it; there are infinitely better ways of making ashtrays and one learns nothing about throwing by fiddling with a sticky palette of clay close to the wheel-head. If this accident happens, as it surely will, the remainder of the clay must be removed (easier to do with the wheel stopped), using a broad palette knife, and a new ball of clay centred.

The beginner soon realises why it is useful to have half a dozen or so balls of clay wedged up for use, and he must not get depressed as one piece after another finds its way into the scraps-bin. Neither clay nor time is wasted. When reconstituted, the clay can be used again, and dozens of mistakes are made before a pot is produced which is worth keeping.

A thin wall near the base simply will not bear the weight of the clay above, and if it does not tear apart it will probably sag like a spare tyre of flesh, or twist into a spiral pattern of ripples as strain is put on the upper part of the pot during shaping. Such a pot is useless—discard it (however much it hurts) by removing it totally from the wheel, and start again. The problem of spiral ripples often occurs when a pot is collared in too rapidly or with too much force. The clay, once widened out into a broad ring, especially near the top of the pot, can only be narrowed down again with patience. If

the ripples appear, start again from scratch, and next time collar
the pot in more gently.

Under-prepared clay, very coarse clay, or indeed any clay at all
may crack around the rim of the pot if it is forced outwards too
quickly. The broken or uneven rim must be corrected immediately,
or the cracks will run right down the pot. A simple technique for
correcting an uneven top is to remove a complete ring of clay as the
pot revolves on the wheel. This is done with a pin or needle with
one end stuck for safety into a cork. By holding the pin on the
outside of the pot in the right hand and pressing it slowly through
the wall of the pot until its point can be clearly felt by a fingertip of
the other hand on the *inside* of the pot, a ring of clay will have been
cut off. By raising the pin firmly, but not too jerkily, the ring can
be lifted off and a new clean rim will be revealed below. This

The technique for levelling an uneven rim.

simple and rather appealing exercise floors some beginners completely because they attempt to lift off the ring too soon, before the point has cut its way through a complete revolution. The method can also be used to level up the top of a pot which has become lopsided through a fault in the centering or opening up. It will, however, be only a temporary expedient as the 'new' rim will indicate by being thicker on one side than the other. More work on the pot will bring up the unevenness again, and each time this happens the top will have to be cut off.

Almost anything can cause the beginner to make mistakes and spoil his pot at this stage. An air bubble trapped in the clay wall like a blister can throw the pot off centre unless it is 'popped' with a pin, with the wheel stationary. Over-jerky movements, especially in releasing the hands from the clay, will set the pot wobbling towards destruction. Wobbles in the wall need not be fatal to the pot—by drawing the clay up again from the bottom with determined steady hands the wobbles can be eliminated, but they must not be neglected as they will only get worse. The beginner's hands will give him sensitivity towards the clay in time, the nerves in the fingertips providing 'feedback' which keeps him informed.

Only practice will give the potter skill, though it helps if he can avoid bad habits. Two things to avoid are sitting with the hands on the pot doing nothing at all, and holding the breath. Beginners spend a great deal of time doing both, often at the same time, which is damaging to both pot and potter. The correct position for the body is forward, with the head above the pot and the elbows resting, if convenient, on the raised rim of the wheel. The picture above shows the position perfectly.

5 Shapes on the wheel

The natural shape which the clay most readily takes up is a plant pot shape, wider at its top than at its base. The discipline of restricting the shape to a cylinder is a good one, though it bores many would-be potters off the wheel. If you can bring yourself to concentrate on this dull shape your mastery of the technique will be quicker. If you cannot resist curved forms, however, it is quite likely that a rather dumpy rounded shape will take over and manage to assert itself in all your pots for a long time to come. Curves which come about by allowing the clay to go the way it wants to go will often sit down, or at least look as if they are going to, and wheel-thrown curves are all the better for being taut and vibrant. Hand techniques, described in Chapters 8 and 9, are more successful for deep, bellying curves.

Many beginners' pots, even the cylindrical variety, have a look of being 'short of clay' or too short overall for their form. Sometimes this is because the top has had to be cut off several times, and always it is because there is just not enough clay in the walls to allow the potter to finish off properly. It is really quite a serious fault, over-come more quickly if one is aware of it, partly because it affects the quality of the rim.

When the hands finally leave the pot at the top, an accent is given to the form as a whole, and character varies enormously according to the final line of the rim. If there is plenty of clay left over the rim can have a full and luscious appearance, and certainly its thickness will give a clue to the thickness of the pot as a whole, and thus to its weight. The tactile appeal of pots is partly to do with their weight—a pot with really winning ways will insist on being picked up—and its weight in the hand should be exactly what one expects from its appearance. A beginner's thin-rimmed pot will give a nasty surprise as it has a thick base and feels like lead, and equally a thin pot should not have too thick a rim or it will feel lighter than it looks. A tight-lipped appearance is sometimes in character with the form as a whole, and so no rules can be formulated about the tops of pots. One should, however, always bear in mind that the rim of a pot, like the muscles of a face, has the ability to give a pot its expression.

Do not be afraid of spending as long on the rim as you have on

the shape as a whole, or of using tools to give a better finish or a contrast between the lip and the outside surface. A small strip of chamois leather held round the profile of the rim will give a very smooth, if impersonal surface. A rubber or metal tool will give an even starker one; a sponge is more gentle, and has the advantage of soaking up the sticky wet clay that often accumulates around the top.

The outside surface of the pot can also be treated or 'finished' with tools. Fingers characteristically leave 'throwing lines' on both the inside and outside, and these are sometimes as personal as handwriting. Large bold throwing lines are often so beautiful and appropriate to a form that to touch them in any way would diminish the pot. A very large thrown pot seems to need its throwing lines to give it 'grain'. On smaller pots they are not always suitable, and a sponge run gently over the surface, as the wheel revolves, will remove them and replace them with its own finer striations. Some potters like to use a rubber or metal tool called a 'kidney' (because of its shape). The rubber tool is sympathetic to the clay and leaves a fine smooth surface—it is especially used for the inside of bowls. The metal one is more difficult to use, but a whole series of metal and wooden tools used on the profile of a thrown pot can achieve forms and surfaces impossible with the fingers. However, there are no nerves in the tips of a tool, as there are in the fingers, to provide a warning to the brain that the clay is uncomfortable and that something is about to go wrong. Sudden death by contortion can come

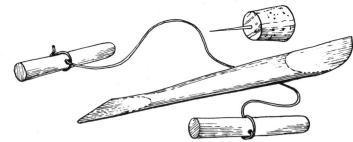

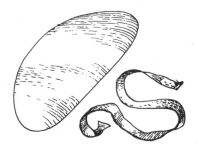

Tools for throwing

Rims can be finished with chamois leather, a sponge or the finger-tips. Varying the position of the fingers produces a variety of rims.

to a pot against which a metal tool is being applied too dry or too harshly.

A pointed metal tool will, if held with its tip against the side of a pot revolving on the wheel, cut a horizontal groove in the wall, but this weakens the wall and should be done only when the walls have an adequate thickness. Such an incised line gives emphasis to the external form, but can also go some way towards concealing a lack of direction or intention in the profile of the pot as made by the fingers, in which case it is a hindrance to the beginner rather than a help.

The drawings overleaf show how a shoulder or waist improves the profile by adding a focus for the eye. Any curve which changes in pitch will be more exciting to the eye than a constant curve. Thus the catenary curve or parabola is literally more dynamic than a semi-circle, and a reversing or ogee curve is more lively if the two opposing parts are not matched. Students of harmony and proportion will make their own experiments in pottery and will be rewarded by the results.

Right: giving a pot hard edges by holding a wooden or metal tool against the wall.

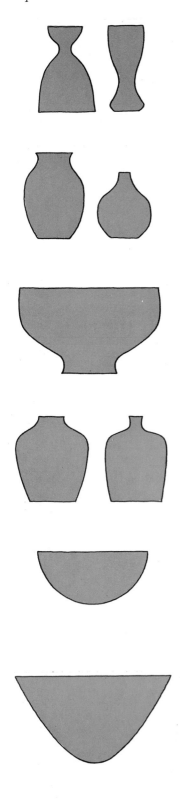

There is no grammar or rulebook of absolutes relating to the form of pots, but it is not difficult when comparing two thrown shapes to see the difference between a strong, clean shape and a hesitant faltering line, or to react to the grace of a curve or the impact of an angular shape. Some pots appear to have personality, even if their character is an unattractive one, and the elements which make up the personality are sometimes hard to define.

When the beginner departs from the cylinder, it is very important for him to have a clear idea in his mind of the shape which he wants to make. An outline or profile drawn with a clayey finger on the workshop wall is a useful guide, and a visible reminder of one's intentions when all is over and done.

No basic pottery shape emphasises harmonic principles more clearly than the open bowl, a popular shape historically, functionally, aesthetically. Certainly beginners' bowls reveal more about their maker's skills and judgements than any other form. A special technique is required to make open bowls on the wheel; it diverges from the 'normal' or upright pot method before the inkwell stage. The potter allows his thumb to make an even curve inside the mound of clay and does not draw the clay towards him, but rather eases it outwards from the start so that the bowl form is obvious from an early stage. The 'drawing up of the wall' is replaced by a stage in which the bowl is progressively increased in height and widened at the same time, with both left and right hands at an angle to the wheel-head. A shallow shape is difficult to make as there is a great deal of unsupported clay around the edges, and it is wise to give the bowl a fairly wide base, some of which can be removed at a later stage (see Chapter 7). As the diameter of the bowl increases so does the speed at which the circumference is revolving, and although the wheel itself should be turning slowly for bowl-making the rate at which the clay is passing through the fingers at the rim is still considerable. To make the point clear, even if the wheel is revolving at only sixty revolutions per minute, the circumference of a 12 inch (30 cm) bowl is passing through the fingers at the rate of about a yard (a metre) a second—too fast for comfort. Pressures from the fingers, if jerky or not maintained, will have an uneven but rapid effect, or to put it another way, a mistake may well mean instant collapse.

With no way of stressing the structure radially, like a cantilevered grandstand, a thrown bowl depends for its stability on its homogeneous body's capacity to withstand gravity. The clay should not be too soft, the rim should not be too fine, the cross-section should taper slightly towards the rim. The thickness of the base of a bowl can with advantage be greater than that of the 'upright' pot. A wide-open shape will appear lighter if it is raised slightly from the surface on which it stands. By removing some of the clay from the base when it is harder the bowl can be given a slight foot. One useful rule to remember when making open or bowl shapes is to keep the form fairly high or 'upright' at the early stages of making; it is much

This sequence of pictures shows how a simple open bowl is made. The hands are drawn from the centre to the edge several times to thin the walls, and are kept locked together for stability.

Throwing a bowl

easier to widen and lower a form from an upright shape than it is to close in a bowl that has been made too wide or too shallow. The final profile of the bowl should be left to the very last stage, and more attention should be given to the inside than to the outside which can be made to match it later on (see Chapter 7). The throwing of a very wide, very shallow bowl requires a great deal of skill—even most experienced potters need to be on the top of their form when making such a bowl—and it requires perfectly prepared clay.

Removing the thrown pot from the wheel-head

The beginner who crosses all hurdles unscathed up to this stage may well meet his downfall now. Removing the thrown shape from the wheel-head seems to induce nervous shivers in the most placid pupil, and unfortunately the essence of the operation is smoothness and confidence.

The inside of the pot is sponged dry of water with the wheel revolving. The fingers remove surplus sticky clay from around the base of the pot, also with the wheel revolving, leaving it as clean as possible. A metal tool can be used if desired to excavate a V-shaped nick around the very base of the pot before stopping the wheel, as a guide to the cutting thread. A nylon thread or double-twisted wire of the kind used in preparing the clay is then pulled underneath the pot as close to the wheel-head as possible, and out at the other side. If the two ends of the wire are crossed over as the wire is being pulled through, the pot will be cut free at once, and can be lifted straight off the wheel, but this requires a certain amount of practice. The beginner may do better to pull the wire through without crossing. A little water is poured on the wheel-head and the operation repeated so that some of the water is pulled under the pot with the wire. This will free the pot from the wheel-head and the pot itself should start to move. The beginner will have looked anxiously inside the pot to see if the wire puts in an appearance on its way through. Pots without bases are not worth keeping and should be destroyed straight away. A slight movement in the clay of the base, however, as the wire passes underneath, is a healthy sign that the base is not too thick.

Throwing small bowls 'from the hump'.

Use a sponge on a wire to remove any water from inside a narrow pot. Make sure the tile is clean, wet and cold before sticking your pot on to it.

Any touching of the finished form with the fingers will mark it, and this should be kept to a minimum. A glazed tile or other smooth surface placed on a level with the wheel-head will help, so that the pot can be slid sideways off the wheel. The tile *must* be clean, cold and wet. If it is dirty, or hot, or dry, or any combination of the three, the pot will stick to it as soon as it makes contact and will be distorted as it is pushed farther on. Similarly, if the pot, when pressed lightly in the direction of the tile with two fingers near to its base refuses to move, it will also be distorted. The wire should be pulled under it again until it is free from the wheel. With one hand holding the tile, one hand pressing against the pot, the whole operation of transferring the pot sideways from wheel to tile should be completed smoothly in about three seconds. Make sure that the tile is being held level and be ready for it to take the weight of the pot. When the pot is completely free from the wheel, lift it away to a place where it will not get bumped casually by other potters, their overalls or their arms, but preferably, if there is space, to a position where it can be seen when you make the next pot. If the pot is allowed to dry on the tile, it will become immovably fastened to it, and it is best to guard against this by running a cutting wire underneath the pot again, on its tile, so that it can dry and shrink without being attached at its base.

Most pots look enormous when they are on the wheel, and shrink to a realistic size when they are on the shelf. They also shrink as they lose moisture, and again in the kiln, all of which has an effect on the self-esteem. Most pots also look very different when seen from the side on the shelf compared to their shape from above during the making, and it is a good thing occasionally to take a sidelong look at an unfinished pot while it is still on the wheel in order to put things back into proportion.

Small pots are easier to take off the wheel-head than big ones; they can be lifted into the air with two fingers of each hand near the base, rather than slid on to tiles, and experienced potters will often make a small pot on top of a large piece of centred clay, cut it through, lift it off and continue throwing 'from the hump' until all the clay is used. Even experienced potters, though, will think twice about sliding or lifting a really large bowl from the wheel-head, as the distortion to the form is often very great. The easiest way of tackling this problem is to stick (with wettish clay) a circular plywood or asbestos disc on to the wheel-head and to make the bowl on top of this, so that it can be lifted off, plywood disc and all, quite simply by loosening the adhesive clay underneath. Clay makes a firm bond between wheel-head and disc by suction but this can be broken when the time comes by holding on to the disc and rotating the wheel. The pot, perfect and undistorted, can then be placed on the shelf with its disc, it is but a good idea to run the wire also under the pot so that it can shrink away from the disc as it dries. If the bowl is not loosened from the disc it will probably never come off in one piece.

Beginners find it difficult to lift a large bowl from the wheel without distorting it. The pictures below show how a disc or bat can be stuck on to the wheel-head and later removed with the pot it bears.

A thrown shape which is complete in itself may need attention as it dries, and the commonest process is that of 'turning' when the pot has become as hard as firm cheese or leather. The whole process of finishing is described in Chapter 7 and the beginner should look there for help in the finishing or leather-hard stage.

Many composite pots like teapots require elements which are made with plastic clay at the wet stage, and for the sake of consistency these are described in the next chapter so that one does not have to dry one's hands only to wet them again.

6 Lids, lips, handles, spouts and composite pots

Many finished pots are the result not of a single wheel-made unit but of several items joined together when the clay has dried to the leather-hard stage. A teapot, for example, consists of a spout and a lid as well as a body and a handle. This chapter ends with the fascinating subject of composite pots—the making of complex sculptural shapes by joining together thrown or hand-made units, but it must inevitably begin with the more work-a-day business of describing lids, lips and spouts, and handles for functional pots. Compared with the general technique of throwing, learning to make all of these extras is very simple indeed. Integrating them into a fine single shape is much harder. The handle must not only fit the hand and be comfortable to hold, but it must also look as though it fits the pot. The lip of a jug must be in character with the shape of the pot it serves. The body of a teapot must only look complete when all its additions have been made.

The 'extras' contribute a good deal to the expression of the pot and each can be made in a variety of ways. By describing in detail first a jug, then a teapot, much of the technique will be covered. The beginner will himself learn the many permutations and is advised to try as many of them as possible.

Lips

Making the pouring lip of a jug is the only positive action which is done with the pot attached to the wheel, and the wheel stationary. It is disarmingly simple. The rim of the pot is stretched and bent outwards by one finger (usually the index finger of the right hand) whilst two fingers (usually the thumb and *second* finger of the left hand) restrain the rim from being too much distorted. The photograph overleaf shows the finger position better than words can describe it. Provided the rim is not treated too roughly, and torn or cracked, an unsatisfactory lip can be erased and the circular rim restored by collaring and working the clay with the wheel in motion again, and the potter can then make another attempt at a lip without discarding the pot.

The index finger which does the stretching should leave as fine

Pulling a lip on a jug.

and sharp an edge as possible on the lip, even if the rim is a thick one. One of the perennial problems for potters and the ceramics industry in general is making a non-drip spout or lip. A drop of liquid will cling readily to a rounded surface when the liquid is being poured and will then run down to the foot when the pot is righted again. The elimination of this most irritating defect often presents the potter with an aesthetic problem, for the best pourers often look strained and ugly. The secret is to make a very fine edge at some point on the lip, even when the shape is a full one. A thick ridge of clay below the rim will often help to give emphasis to the line of the pulled lip by underlining it, and this ridge forms an aesthetically attractive attachment point for the handle (see page 44). The rate at which the liquid is funnelled towards the lip will also affect a jug's pouring qualities, and the funnelling effect is increased if, during the making of the lip, the two fingers of the left hand are used firmly.

By pulling back with these two fingers as the lip is drawn forwards, the surface of the rim will be made undulating, which often gives the pot more dignity. The beginner should practise with many shapes and compare his results to the 'cut' lip method. This involves placing a folded triangle of soft clay against a cutaway form in the rim of the pot and attaching it in the same way as for spouts and handles.

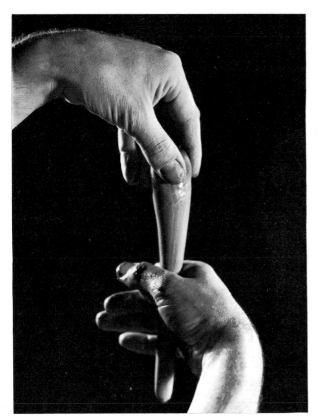

Above: pulling a handle. Right: pulled handles are stuck on a board to dry a little.

Handles

On wheel-made pots handles are best made by the pulling method. This obliges the potter to take a piece of clay of throwing consistency shaped like a carrot, to hold it firmly in one hand, and stroke it downwards with the other, rather like milking a cow. Constant lubrication with water makes it sensible to pull handles near the sink, although on large pots they are best made on the work bench by attaching the raw clay carrot direct to the pot at the desired attachment point by scoring the leather-hard pot's surface with a pin, adding a little water, and pressing the thick end of the carrot on to it. The pot in question has to be stout and firm enough not to be distorted when the handle is pulled out to shape, and best results are achieved if the pot can be held at an angle and the handle

41

pulled downwards. Large handles 'pulled from the pot' appear to grow out of their source naturally, and when the handle is the correct length and thickness it can be bent over and attached at the base with the pressure of two thumbs. If the handle is too long the extra length should be broken off before attachment. The shape can be modified slightly after the handle is attached, but bending or squeezing of the shape usually spoils the 'arch' and finishing is best confined to the two attachment points.

The bottom of the handle should never be made thinner than the top. Practice will teach the puller how to regulate the squeeze so that the handle is slightly slimmer at the centre than at the two ends. Pulling the handle direct on the pot is suitable also for small lugs on large jars, and for the kind of handle which sticks straight out like a lever. A straight handle can occasionally be used on a pot such as a coffee or milk jug. In use it is only practical if the handle springs from a little lower than half way down the pot, so that the weight is counter-balanced about the handle as it is turned.

Beginners usually make handles for their pots separately as shown here. Handles should never be made in isolation, away from the pots which they are going to fit. If the potter keeps his eye on the pot he is more likely to make a handle of the right size and shape. The cross section of the handle, made in the deep crook of the hand between the thumb and the forefinger, can be made symmetrical by turning the handle round through 180° so that both sides of the handle in turn meet the 'crook' (see drawing).

Like throwing lines on the side of a pot, handle profiles are as personal as handwriting and most beginners take time to become fluent. Basic rules to remember are always to make sure you have

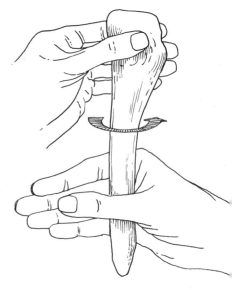

By turning the left hand and the clay it is holding through 180° the cross-section of the handle can be made symmetrical.

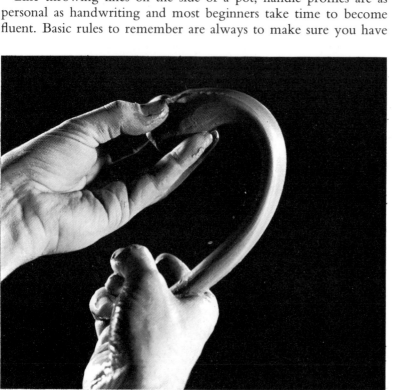

Test the shape and size of the handle before attaching it.

enough clay in the carrot for the handle required, leaving a healthy lump at the top by which to grasp it while it is being made. Too many handles slip to the floor at this stage. When the shape is right, attach the handle firmly to a horizontal surface, letting it hang down like a dog's tail to dry a little before attachment. Finally, always make at least twice as many handles as you need to allow for accidents at the attachment stage. Many handles are forgotten in the pressure of events during an evening class, and go too hard to be used. To test for hardness, remember that the handle, hanging nearly straight downwards, should be capable of being bent to the appropriate arc without cracking across, but should not be so wet that it responds stickily to handling.

Taking a suitable candidate from its sticking place, remove the unshaped lump at the top end with the ball of the thumb. This makes a slightly concave shape well adapted to the curve of the pot. The concave face should be textured by scoring lines or making small holes with the point of a sharp pencil. It is now ready to be married to a correspondingly scored surface on the wall of the pot. A little water squeezed from a sponge on to both surfaces will help to make the bond a firm one, and water is a better adhesive than sticky clay or 'slip', though some potters keep bowls of sticky clay especially for this purpose. If the jug or pot is held 'face downwards', the lower attachment can be made by allowing the handle to arch over, pressing the end down with two thumbs. This fixes the handle to a ready roughened and moistened attachment point, and at the same time breaks off any superfluous length. Beware too great a pressure, which can injure the shape of even a leather-hard pot, and take care too that the upper attachment does not spoil the circularity of the rim. It is important to ensure that the handle of a jug with a lip or spout is exactly opposite the lip or spout, or pouring becomes a messy business, and it is important to check too that the handle, when seen from above, sticks straight out. If it is bent (see diagram) it will be uncomfortable in the hand.

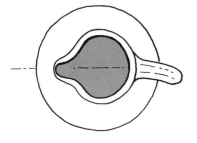

Handles should stick straight out.

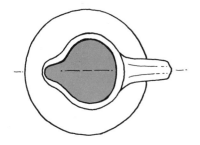

Attaching a handle.

Beginners find that pulled handles often break in the pulling and a common fault is to make a handle which tapers too much to a point. Early attempts are often lumpy and a disgrace to the pots, but the beginner can take comfort; the technique of making perfect handles becomes apparent with practice. They can also be made by the casting method (see Chapter 11) and by the ingenious method of pulling an oval loop of a very stiff wire, like a monocle on a stick but without the glass, through a block of wedged clay. This will release an even strip of clay, the profile of which can be adjusted by changing the shape of the wire loop. Try it. The handles are perfectly uniform and can be used more quickly after making than the hand-pulled ones, but they have little individuality and no soul. Circular handles with a similar lack of sensitivity can be made by slicing a thrown cylinder into rings and attaching a ring, like an ear, to the side of the pot.

A potter can spend a lifetime making jugs alone, fruitfully varying the size and relationships of handles and lips. As an object, the jug has a very strong appeal because it is totally self-justifying, and it is recommended for beginners. As a basic storage vessel, adapted for the transfer of its contents, it is a fundamental domestic requirement, and puts in an appearance at all stages of civilisation. Museum collections of medieval ware often include jugs and pitchers which are perfect forms, however coarse grained; industrially produced jugs are often gawky or downright ugly by comparison, although in the 1930s and again in recent years they have often been the focus of much ingenuity and wit.

A ridge under the lip makes a pot look more decisive and the handle look more natural.

Lids

When the beginner can tackle a teapot he is really making progress, for this is the most complicated everyday pot. The basic form must be made to accommodate a lid, which should not fall out when the pot is tilted. Lid and spout should be made at the same time as the body of the pot; the handle made later. A suitable body for a teapot may well look rather dumpy without its additions; it will certainly have a specialised rim, usually with a recess into which the lid can nestle. This recess is made simply, in a few seconds, towards the end of the making of the teapot body. Rather more clay than usual is kept at the top of the shape, and the rim is flattened with the index finger of the right hand. The thumb nail on the left hand is then brought vertically down to split this rim in the middle, and a little downwards pressure makes a step in the rim. The edge of the recess should not be too fine and thin, though its profile should be fairly square and it should slope downwards slightly towards the centre. If the shape of the recess is an awkward one it may well be difficult to clean. The thumb and thumbnail are the most sensitive tools for this operation, though a wooden modelling tool can be substituted if the thumbnail is outrageously the wrong shape. Very

Making a recess to hold the teapot lid is very easy. Flatten the top first, then 'split' it with the thumbnail. The index finger of the right hand has a key function in holding the outside steady so that the top will keep its shape as the recess is made.

long fingernails are a considerable encumbrance when making pottery, and very short ones are also unhelpful.

A chamois leather is useful for rounding off the inside edge of the recess, and the outside profile of the pot should be checked after the downward pressure of recess-making. It is difficult, however, to do further work on the inside of the pot without damaging this recess.

When the pot is removed from the wheel, two measurements should be taken straight away with calipers. These measurements give the correct width for the lid and for its 'throat'. Only one pair of calipers is needed. The measurements can be 'stored' by pressing the caliper tips into a piece of plastic clay.

The teapot's lid should be thrown on the wheel straight after the body of the pot and made from the same kind of clay, to ensure the same colour and shrinkage. It will need a throat to stop it falling out of the pot as the tea is poured and, traditionally, it should also have a small hole to let out the steam. The top will need a graspable knob and the lid will be finished by turning (see Chapter 7). If the lid is made upside down on the wheel, the throat is made by hollowing the middle first, then the outside, and its diameter can be altered to match the caliper measurement. This is all much easier to do than it looks. If the top side is uppermost on the wheel, a knob can easily be isolated by pressure with the thumbs slightly away from the centre, raising a lump in the centre. A lid made the 'right way up' on the wheel needs a very thick base, as the throat will have to be made out of this at the leather-hard stage. It is rather a long-winded

Making a teapot lid upside down on the wheel.

business, and for quantity production lids are usually designed so that they can be made quickly with little follow-up work. The design and technique, however, must relate to the form of the mother pot. The profile of the lid must continue or complement the pot as a whole and the potter should be able to see the main body of the pot while making the lid so the two are in sympathy. Lids made in isolation rarely look right when the pot is assembled. If the lid needs to be sharply arched, then it can be made upside down in the form of a bowl, perhaps flattening towards the rim, and its knob added later. Similarly, the lid can be made like a sort of beehive, the right way up. The various drawings show several different types which look complicated but are in fact very easy to make. Less easy is getting the size right—the lid should fit snugly with limited play in its recess. Neither is it easy to produce a knob which suits an elegant small teapot, but which is substantial enough to hold and robust enough not to break in the washing-up bowl.

There is no limit to the possible variations, though not all of them are practical. The higher the lid the more unstable when the pot is tilted, the smaller the knob, the less insulation it will provide for the fingers, and teapot lids can become very hot. The knob itself can be added by throwing when the rest of the lid has become leather-hard. A small ball of throwing clay will stick easily to the centre of the lid and, using a very little water, a knob can be shaped on the wheel, and any extra clay cut off (see page 62).

Pots other than teapots have different requirements for lids, and the drawings show several varieties. It is useful for storage jars to have lids which are flush with the top of the pot, or have a recessed

Use calipers to measure the maximum available for the throat of the lid.

Lids for teapots, coffee pots and jars

Throwing a lid with its knob uppermost.

knob to help stacking. Rarely can ceramic lids be airtight unless they are aided with rubber or cork washers, and where hygiene is important, as in jam or mustard pots, it is a good idea to avoid profiles which are difficult to clean. Overlapping lids may be the most suitable here. Really wide lids for casseroles should be made on circular bats as described in the section on throwing a bowl, so that they can be removed from the wheel without distortion. It is the casserole lid which, manipulated as it needs to be in a hot and hostile oven, most usually falls short of the ideal. It needs to have a really large knob which can be grasped, even through an oven glove, and at the same time it needs to be low or it is sure to tangle with the shelf above. Casserole bodies often have small lugs on the sides to help the cook, but the most helpful lid is one which can be

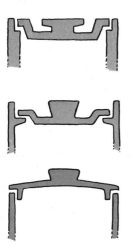

The lugs on the sides of this casserole are cut from thrown cylinders.

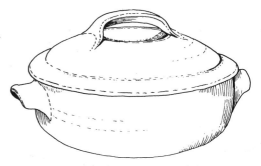

lifted from the side, without falling off the casserole base. The casserole in the diagram below shows a simple solution designed by Michael Casson.

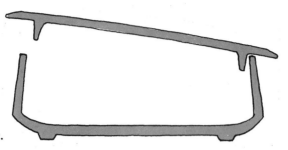

A casserole lid held in place by its throat.

Spouts

Our teapot still needs a spout, and this can be made by casting (see Chapter 11) or throwing. Any other hand method will probably be too crude for this delicate job. It is quite simple to throw a small hollow concave shape like a miniature cooling tower, using clay

Throwing a spout

The rim of this pot by Hans Coper was squeezed into an elliptical shape after throwing.

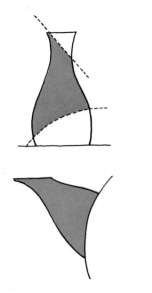

Two cuts at an angle are needed to finish the thrown spout.

from the top of a centred lump. Open the clay with the thumb as usual but only use the smallest finger of the left hand inside for drawing up or the spout will become too big and clumsy. Finish the lip with a small outward curve, and cut through the pot near its base, lifting off the small tube and storing it on a tile. As with handles it is wise to make rather more spouts than one will need so that there is always a spare in case of accidents. Throwing on the wheel is the easiest part of the operation of making a spout. When it is leather-hard the wider lower part must be cut at an angle with a sharp knife to fit the belly of the pot body. The spout should then be placed roughly in position and a fine outline scratched on the pot around the edge of the spout. A metal drill-bit of approximately $\frac{3}{16}$ inch (5 mm) diameter should be used to make the holes which will restrain the tealeaves, and this should be done by twisting the bit with the fingers with great care, with a hand or finger on the inside of the wall to prevent the wall from giving way.

The pouring end of the spout can also be cut at an angle, as shown in the diagram, although cutting it is not always necessary. A scored surface on both the pot and the base of the spout is needed to make a good bond and the two should be pressed firmly together with a little water on the contact surfaces. A comic and catastrophic fault is that of making the level of the top of the spout lower than that of the lid, so that the pot can be filled to the point where tea gushes from the spout without any tilting. The spout on the teapot shown overleaf is only just high enough to prevent this.

Spouts can be used on drinking flasks as well as tea and coffee pots; handles and lids on a great variety of pots. These items and the techniques described for making them and attaching them can also be applied purely as decoration, but if they are to be practical they must function properly and feel right in the hand.

Composite pots

A composite pot is the result of joining together units which were made separately. The elements may all be made on the wheel, or some may be hand produced or cast. An advantage of the composite pot is that it extends the potter's capabilities beyond the working limits of the wheel. Thrown cylinders can be joined to make towers many feet high. Thrown pieces can be cut up and set at right angles to the main axis or rearranged completely into sculptural structures.

The technique is extremely simple. Thrown pieces are cut when leather-hard with a sharp knife, the contact surfaces are roughened or scored and joined together with a little water. Clay is heavy, of course, and gravity is an important factor in design. Occasionally composite pots may gain by appearing to defy gravity, but it is not practical for ceramics which are to be handled or used to have a high centre of gravity or an unstable shape.

It is possible, with a great deal of patience, to throw an onion-shaped pot like those shown opposite all in one piece, but soft

clay will make such a shape unstable on the wheel, and the failure rate will be very high. It is much more practical to make two forms, joining them when the clay is hard enough to bear the weight.

Provided composite pots retain a single axis, they can be completed on a revolving wheel with the use of a metal or wooden tool (see Chapter 7) to smooth the join or even by 'throwing' a ring of clay over the joined areas. The concept is straight-forward in practice though difficult to explain. If a sausage of throwing clay is carefully arranged around the pot as a complete ring at the junction between the two thrown units, it can be worked with the hands using very little water, just as a foot ring can be thrown on an upturned bowl, and the join can be made perfect.

Aesthetic problems which emerge from the composite technique are all-absorbing. How to relate two dissimilar and distinctive shapes into a satisfactory unit is a good exercise for the serious student, and they may occupy him for years or for a lifetime. He will soon find that although the technique is simple it is difficult to combine shapes harmoniously. When he succeeds his composite pots will have a vibrant tension quite unlike that of a pot which is made in one piece. Thrown pots should be relaxed but composite pots can gain by this tension and the technique provides an opportunity for a potter's work to change its pitch, and to increase its scale.

Make sure the mouth of the spout is higher than the level of the tea in the pot.

When making several pots the same size, it is helpful to fix a pointer to the side of the wheelhead with a lump of clay, to indicate the correct diameter for the rim.

7 Turning, finishing and fettling

Turning the base of the bowl on the wheel.

When the pot has been removed from the wheel it can be allowed to dry completely and can be fired in the kiln without further addition. More usually, there is work to be done on the pot as it dries. It can be altered in plan or squeezed while it is still wet: for example the lip of a jug is made on the wheel as soon as the pot is complete. Most of the work of cleaning up or 'fettling' the pot, however, is done when the pot has dried to the 'leather-hard' stage. 'Leather' or 'cheese' hard is fairly self-explanatory: clay in this stage can be picked up and handled without damaging the shape; it can be pared easily with a knife. If the parings flake into small pieces instead of staying in long strips like apple peelings then it is too hard. If the wall of the pot gives to gentle pressure, then it is too soft.

The drying of the pot must be carefully controlled and should not be hurried. If directional heat is applied to a pot, the shape will be distorted as one side dries more quickly than the other, and this is irretrievable. The exposed parts of a pot will normally dry more quickly than the base, and to prevent strains and over-drying of the rim of a bowl it is a good idea to turn it upside down when the rim has become firm enough to support the pot's weight, as this will halt the drying of the rim and expose the base to the air.

Pots which have dried out completely cannot be turned, and damping down pots which have become too dry, by soaking them briefly under the tap, or immersing them for a second or two in a bowl of water, is a risky business. Ideally the pot should be caught at exactly the right leather-hard stage, and this poses a serious problem for the once-a-week evening student. Most potters have 'damp cupboards' which should be airtight to keep the moisture in, but all too often are left with doors open. In damp November a pot may take a week or so to dry, depending on its size and thickness, but in summer a few hours is enough to dry a freshly thrown pot to the leather-hard stage. If a pot can only be attended to at weekly intervals, a fairly airtight biscuit tin is an essential part of the beginner's personal equipment as in this a damp state can be maintained for longer periods. The trouble with a biscuit tin, of course, is that its contents are invisible from outside and may be damaged if it is carelessly handled. A better though more expensive expedient for the protection of one's pots is a rigid translucent and airtight plastic container, which is a little more likely to be handled with respect.

Pots are very vulnerable at all stages until they have been fired in the kiln, and any contact with any surface of a damp pot will leave its mark. A simple block of wood can be employed to square off the sides of a freshly thrown bowl, a bamboo tool or a specially shaped cutter can be used to make flutes when the pot is still wet or as it dries. Any impressing of the clay with seals, etc. must be left until the clay, like leather, is tough enough not to give way to pressure.

At the leather-hard stage, the accessories—spouts, handles, lids etc—are fixed to the mother pot, and thrown items can be assembled to make the composite pots described in Chapter 6. Most

people associate the leather-hard stage with *turning*. In this process the pot is placed again on the wheel and metal tools are used to remove surplus clay. The process can be a creative one, the entire form being refined, inside and out, with a turning tool, but more usually it is a corrective one, especially for the beginner, improving the shape of the base of the pot by cutting away clay.

Turning is a slower process than throwing, and often beginners will spend half an hour or more turning a pot which has taken only two or three minutes to throw. For a corrective process, this is quite ridiculous. Several new pots could have been thrown in the same time, and the potter would have made more progress. The beginner should try to avoid the pitfall of throwing crudely, and then trying to turn some aesthetic quality into the pot at the leather-hard stage. In classes, laborious turning can monopolise wheels for hours on end, with a bad effect on everyone's nerves.

There is nothing sacred about turning; it is not an inevitable ritual. The pot should be judged for shape and weight as it stands. Only if it is found wanting should it be turned. Very simple forms, if they are well thrown, need no turning at all.

Common practice is to use kick wheels for turning, reserving electric wheels for throwing. If an electric wheel is available, however, it is equally suitable, and will probably help to get the job done quickly. As with throwing, turning involves fixing the object centrally on the wheel, working on it and removing it, and each stage has its minor hazards. Most open shapes will be fixed to the wheel upside down, and the rim of the pot, so carefully made, is now in contact with the metal wheel-head where it can be easily damaged. If the wheel-head is too wet, the rim may soften and buckle. If the wheel-head is completely dry the pot will have to be held in place by means of a long sausage of throwing clay, like a rampart around the pot, or by a trio of lumps of clay— perhaps a little harder than one would use for throwing—pressed against the rim. The pot must be precisely on the centre and a good start towards achieving this is to make a series of concentric circles on a damp wheel-head with a fingernail. If these temporary rings are about $\frac{1}{4}$ inch apart, one of the circles is bound to correspond closely to the rim of the pot, and it can be carefully positioned and the wedges or sausages added. Many experienced potters will dispense with these buttresses and rely on the natural adhesion of a damp rim to a damp wheel-head, but the beginner is strongly advised to use them, taking care not to buckle or distort the rim with too much sideways pressure. It is maddening when turning a pot to see it fly off the wheel-head and crumple up in the wheel tray. To avoid this it must be firmly fixed on the head, and supported. A disc of fairly hard clay completely covering the wheel-head, and completely level, can be used as a bed for very vulnerable or fine rims. Clay is kinder to rims than the hard metal of the wheel-head, but it must be firm enough not to stick permanently to a pot being turned, and sometimes a dusting of powdered clay

Dampen the wheel-head and the pot only very sparingly, to avoid damage to the rim.

between the turning 'bed' and the pot itself will usefully reduce adhesion.

Inversion of the pot allows its true base, inaccessible during the throwing, to be shaped, and this is particularly important for bowls. Vertical shapes, however, do not always need to have a concave or hollow foot, and if any tidying up is necessary around the base, it can be done with the pot the right way up on the wheel. If it is necessary, in order to make a foot ring or for some special purpose, to invert a tall slender shape, there is immediately a problem of stability on the wheel, and the usual method is to prepare a 'chuck' or recessed bed on the wheel-head. Clay is used for this chuck, and it should be a little harder than throwing clay. It is not necessary to centre the clay for the chuck but the clay must be levelled at the top without using water with a metal tool like a steel ruler, and a centred hollow should then be made to accommodate the top of the inverted pot. A perfect 'female' shape is rarely possible, as the diagram shows, but it is essential that it should grip the pot firmly and hold it so that it is truly vertical. The hollow centre of the chuck should be made with a sharp metal tool instead of with the fingers. It is not necessary to use the same kind of clay for the chuck as was used in the pot itself. It is wise, however, to use a smooth ungrogged clay for this purpose, as coarse clay can be scratchy, and a dark coloured clay used for a chuck will occasionally stain a pot which is made of white clay (or vice versa) and so too big a contrast between the clays should be avoided.

Sometimes a tall pot to be turned can be inverted and lowered into the neck of a fired pot, itself fixed to the wheel with a ring of clay. This gives greater stability than a chuck when the load becomes top-heavy. Occasionally the diameter of a bowl's rim will be greater than that of the wheel-head, and when inverted it will be very difficult to 'hang' it over the wheel without damage. In such a case, a centred lump of hardish clay, matching as closely as possible the inside profile of the bowl, should be used to grip the bowl firmly on the wheel, or a ring of clay used to cushion the wheel's edge (see diagram).

Leather-hard pots put on the wheel for turning must be centred, and running true. You can tell if a pot is off-centre when the wheel is revolving because it will wobble, but the wobble is hard to see

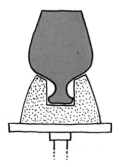

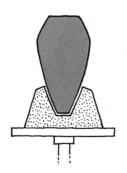

'Chucks' for turning

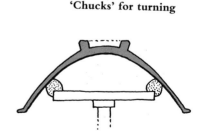

   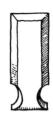 

when the wheel is brought to a stop to correct the fault. To check if a pot is on centre bring the point of a needle or pointed turning tool towards its surface at its widest part as it revolves. Stop the wheel when the point has made contact with the clay. If the resulting scratch mark runs right around the pot, then the pot is truly centred, but if it is only a short cut then the pot is clearly out of true and the pot should be pushed *away* from the centre of the curved scratch. How far to push it? Experience will tell, but it is usually less than you think. Adjust the clay wedges around the pot before you begin again. Hopefully the pot will now be running true, but check for centre again by the same method, and even if it takes several attempts do not start to cut away the clay until you are sure that the pot is running true.

Turning can be done with any tool capable of cutting through clay and a variety of materials is made and sold for this purpose. Some of the popular shapes are drawn above. Personal preferences vary enormously and it is quite likely that a broken or sharpened kitchen knife will outstrip all manufactured versions as a favourite. Most tools, however, have blades at right angles to their handles and all of them are better if they are sharp. Tools with a convex profile are the only ones which will carve out hollow curves, and straight-edged tools are better for convex shapes and straight sides. A minimum requirement, therefore, is one of each sort. Tools made of very heavy metal bring their weight to bear on the pot and, like heavy screwdrivers, they make light work. Wire-loop turning tools cannot be heavy but the wire at least must be very strong and not springy.

Most beginners learn to turn with the tools which are available at an evening class. The inevitable wetness and untidiness of the working area of potteries makes them rust quickly, and they seem to get lost very quickly. If you go to an evening class with only one tool of your own, let it be a sharp turning tool, and make sure you put your name on it.

Before starting to cut away the clay you must have tested the thickness of your pot. How thick is it in the base? With a bowl it is easy to tell, simply by feeling both sides at once and deducing how far apart are your fingertips. With an enclosed pot it is less easy, though a needle point pressed through the base will give some idea by its resistance how long it takes to go through the bottom, and a

A needle or a fingertip held steady as the pot revolves will indicate if it is centred.

The left hand can be arched around the pot to catch it if it jumps off the wheel during turning.

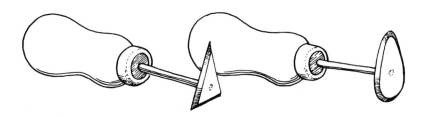

Tools for turning

pinprick of these dimensions will soon fill in during the turning process. Once the pot is inverted on the wheel there is no way of telling how thick the bottom is except by pressing it. Tapping the bottom provides information rather too late, because its note is dull whilst the pot is thick in the base, and changes its pitch only when it becomes membrane-thin, inappropriately thin for any pot. Most beginners turn their way right through the bases of several pots, and as soon as a hole appears they must discard the pot. Repairs can be made by adding clay of the same consistency, but it is better to learn to turn correctly than to learn to make repairs.

With many upright pottery shapes, carving clay from the underneath of the pot is quite unnecessary, but it is usually helpful with bowls so that the outside profile of the bowl can follow the inside profile. The very base of the bowl thus remains convex like an egg, and the bowl stands on a foot ring which is left when the clay within it has been turned away. It is sensible to mark with two fine incisions the position of this foot ring on the upturned base, and to cut away the clay on the outside first and then in the centre, leaving the foot ring as a projecting ridge. This order is important, because it allows the outside profile to be determined precisely and satisfactorily without boats having been burned.

Foot rings for bowls and other pots can have many different characters. They lift the main form up from the surface on which it stands, and this always lightens the appearance of the pot, but the potter should experiment with outward turning, vertical, broad and narrow profiles in the foot ring, and study if possible Oriental examples, which cannot be bettered for harmony with the form they have to carry. Small high foot rings are often elegant and graceful, but wide low ones are usually more practical and stable.

Always work on the right hand side of the pot, as in throwing,

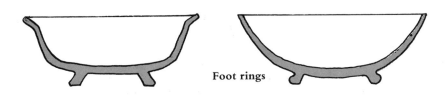

Foot rings

Two lines are incised on the bottom of a bowl to indicate the outside and inside edges of the footring, before the turning is begun.

and hold the tool in the right hand, steadying the blade if possible with one of the fingers of the left hand. The rest of the left hand can sometimes be cupped around the form ready to catch it if it decides to jump off the wheel-head. The angle at which the blade meets the clay of the pot is important. The best angle will soon be obvious from experiment but it certainly will be an acute angle, much less than 90°, so that in effect the cutting edge is dragging clay from the pot rather than stabbing into it. A tool held at the wrong angle may bounce rhythmically and uncontrollably against the clay, making ripples like ripples on sand, and these are called 'chatter markings'. Invariably ugly, they are sometimes tiresomely difficult to remove. As soon as they begin to appear the beginner must stop work, and find a remedy. Blunt tools and dry clay are frequent causes of chatter marks, as is the use of the wrong angle or too wide an area of the turning tool blade. Sharpening the tool, dampening the clay with a wet sponge and changing the position and angle of the tool will help to remove the marks and restore a smooth surface.

The surface created by the turning tool is inevitably different from the one your fingers make in throwing, and a pot which changes texture at some point on its profile often suffers as a result. The whole profile can be turned lightly to remove this inconsistency, but such a form loses its life and looks more mechanical than when it showed the marks of throwing. It is best to keep the turning to a minimum on the side of a pot and to learn to make the merging of the two surface textures as sensitively as possible.

The base as thrown on the wheel, with the inevitable fingermarks left after it has been removed from the wheel, is often a more appropriate shape than a neatly turned base. A few minutes work with a turning tool on the side of a pot can transform the proportions and, alas, this is very often for the worse. Because it is difficult to assess the effect one is having on the proportions of something which is upside down, a pot which is to be inverted for turning should be studied carefully before the process begins, and any change to its profile planned in advance of starting the work. It is vital in the finished pot, however, that no really sharp edges come into contact with a table or other surface on which

Below left: giving a cylinder a slightly recessed base. When complete, the hard corner is softened with the tool to prevent its being too sharp. Right: the profile of the bowl has been made convex to follow the inside curve. If a heavy tool is rested on the foot ring you can see if there is enough clearance for the base, but if the tool wobbles as the pot goes round the foot ring is uneven and further work is needed.

the form will finally stand. Glaze on a sharp edge can be as sharp as broken glass when it is fired and will cut hands and certainly scratch tables. All 'corners' should therefore be rounded off to avoid these sharp edges, but the rounding is effective if only very slight, and crisp hard-edged forms do not need to look softened by this necessary act.

The leather-hard stage is the final stage at which major changes may be made to a pot's surface and these include incised designs, fluting, perforations and the application of slips (see Chapter 16).

When the pot has become completely dry it is fragile, brittle and no longer cold to the touch. In its unfired state the pot is known as 'green'. Handled carefully a dry 'green' pot can be sandpapered. This is another corrective process which in certain respects replaces turning, though it is much slower. The effect of sandpaper on the exposed surfaces is almost always unpleasant as the material is insensitive and attractive marks made in the throwing are quicky rubbed away. Fine sandpaper can be useful in smoothing joints of spouts and handles, but again only as a corrective measure. The most sensible use of sandpaper is smoothing the uneven bottoms of pots which have not been turned. If the sandpaper is rubbed on the pot's base, the base will probably be rounded and the fault will be aggravated. If the sandpaper is fixed on a table and the pot rubbed on it, the surface of the base will be made smooth and the pot will stand firm. Loose grains of sand or grog on a hard smooth surface such as slate makes an even better abrasive combination for the base of a pot, and if the green pot is ground carefully with a circular motion onto this the base of the pot will quickly be made level. Experienced potters have learned by making mistakes how vulnerable green pots are to breakage. They will *never* pick up an unfired teapot or teacup by its handle, or a bowl by its edge. Beginners often do just this, and the pot breaks. At this stage in its life a pot cannot be repaired and the effort of making it is wasted.

When turning a lid, first make concentric cuts on a pad of clay. Carve out a groove to match the throat of the lid with a pointed tool and make sure the lid fits snugly before turning begins (below right). The knob can be added as a small ball of clay (bottom left) and then shaped to suit the pot.

8 Hand made pottery:

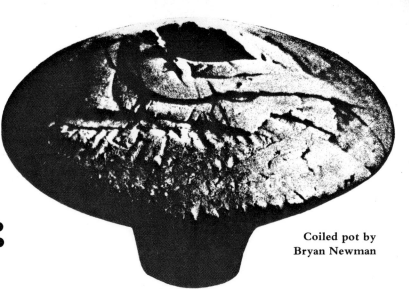

Coiled pot by Bryan Newman

Coiling

It is a humbling experience to visit a gallery of African pottery such as that at Burlington House, London, and to be confronted by pots so powerful and perfect, made for everyday use, by hand.

Whilst the wheel as a technical device gives speed, precision and imposes a discipline, there is no question of its having elbowed hand-made ceramics into second place as far as worth and beauty are concerned. The would-be potter without a wheel must never for a moment feel he lacks facilities to make pots. He may rightly feel some trepidation since, armed with a simple technique and the simplest of tools, he is entering the arena from which have emerged many of the world's greatest potters.

Alas, many evening classes are so short of wheels that teachers often introduce pupils to pottery by starting them on hand-made shapes. The implication of this is not only that the technique but the *concept* is for the novice. Added to this is the inevitable association in a classroom between working clay by hand and 'play-clay' of kindergarten. To be introduced as a beginner to the hand-shaping processes when one has not become familiar with the characteristics of clay on the wheel is no fun. Clay will crack, sag, stiffen and stick to the table. It will appear obtuse and messy, and reluctant to yield up any reward. The sooner one can come to terms with it by mastering it on the wheel the better. At the same time, given the fact of limited wheel facilities, one must accept that many beginners are obliged to start with hand-made pottery, and I hope that this chapter will be helpful to them.

There are several minor techniques of hand-building, and two principal ones, both evilly named. *Coiled* pottery allows the potter the freedom to build really large pots, as big as the kiln will allow, and *slab* building allows him to use hard-edged forms and plane surfaces of infinite variety.

Coiling, the traditional method of many African potters, as shown below, usually produces pots which are circular in cross-section, or which approximate to a radial symmetry, like an apple or a gourd. It is an apt simile, for of all pottery techniques this is the most organic. It does not lend itself to precision any more than the beauty of a woman or a whale can be invoked by following rules or numbers. The technique obeys natural laws of gravity (unlike throwing which is often helped by centrifugal force to defy them) and has a more direct relationship between its texture and its form than other methods. The potter makes a number of long rolls of clay, circular and solid in cross-section. These are called 'coils' (though they are not twisted in any way) and laid in rings one on top of another they form the walls of the pot. Shape is controlled by the size of the ring.

Clay for making a coil pot is prepared in the same way as for throwing, although very plastic throwing clay is not necessary for this technique and most potters prefer a coarse grogged or sanded clay which will have a better 'tooth' and texture. A favourite clay for coiled pots is called *Crank mixture*, originally prepared for making the 'saggers' or protective drums in open-flame kilns. It is cheap and coarse to the point of being abrasive. Red clay is also popularly used for coiled pots, and is better if it includes grog.

The African method of coiling and (right) some of the organic forms the method produces.

Obviously the pot must be made throughout with the same clay, and it is important to provide oneself with enough clay to finish the job. Coiling is one of the slowest methods of making pots, and the student at the once-weekly class may well spend three weeks or so on a pot. He must put his store of clay away in an airtight bag with his work each week, or he may find the clay in the bins is of a different colour and type in the next session.

The technique of making coils is shown below. Both the diameter of the sausage and its length are important. It is not wise to make coils less than $\frac{3}{8}$ inch (1 cm) in diameter, and it is not practical to roll them under the hands when the length exceeds about 18 inches (45 cm). The width of one's hands placed fingers outstretched side by side so that the thumbs just touch indicates the maximum length of clay one can control. If the roll of clay is wider than this, the coil will become twisted up and will probably break, as only the clay under one's fingers rotates with rolling. A lump of clay the size of a

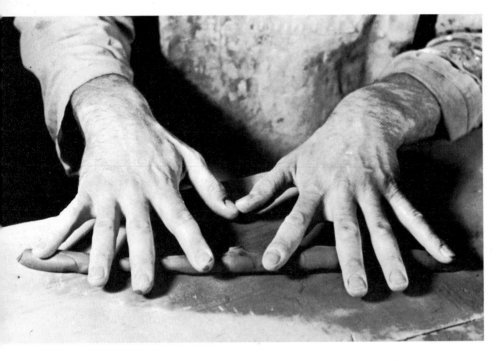

healthy carrot will make a roll of sensible length and the potter will make about seven or eight rolls before beginning the pot. To make more is a mistake, however, as rolls dry very quickly, especially if laid on a wooden table, and as soon as they are too stiff to bend freely they are useless and must be put in the scraps-bin. In some primitive societies potters walk backwards around the pot, feeding out clay like a hosepipe onto the wall, but in confined spaces and certainly for smaller pots it is a help if the pot itself can be rotated as it is being made. The ideal help here is a 'banding' wheel made of heavy cast iron in two parts. Most potteries have them, and mostly they get broken as beginners lift them from bench to bench without realising that the bottom will fall out and smash expensively on the floor. Without a banding wheel the wheel-head of a kick wheel will do. Failing that a biscuit tin or any solid box placed on the bench to raise the pot up to a better working height will serve, and by moving the box around the pot can be turned on the bench without itself being touched.

Use both hands together to roll a sausage of clay into a long, even coil. Try to make coils of consistent diameter; they need not be perfectly round.

Joining up
the coils

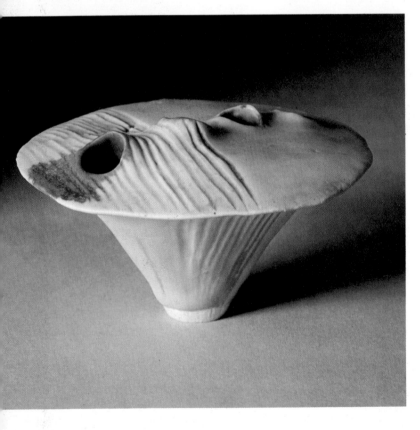

Top: composite pots by Hans Coper. Each form is thrown in two pieces, squeezed and joined when leather hard. The outside is coated with brown and white slip. Above and left: hand-made pots by Ruth Duckworth. The small form on the left is made from porcelain clay, pinched into shape as described on page 83. The two pots above are made from coils, and are as big as pumpkins.

Most potters make the base of a coil pot by rolling out a disc of clay with an ordinary rolling pin. Silver sand or grog, canvas or simply a piece of newspaper should be put underneath the clay to prevent it sticking to the table whilst it is being rolled out. If the clay sticks to the rolling pin it is too soft, and firmer clay should be used, or the lump dried out. If the pot is to be circular a true circle should be made on the disc with compasses or a point on the end of a string and the surplus clay cut away. Do resist the temptation to draw round some handy plate, as this will fix the size of the base and will almost certainly not be the size you require. The thickness of the rolled-out disc should be the same as the diameter as the rolls of clay and certainly should not be less than $\frac{3}{8}$ inch (1 cm). A roll of clay is pressed onto the base as a complete ring and further rings are added to this. No 'glue' is required, just pressure from the fingers

and the rolls will stick to one another. It is not a good method to use a continuous spiral of clay, as in this way the top of the pot will never be level, but continuously mounting. It is not at all necessary to have complete rings of clay each time, as small lengths can be added with ease to fill in the gaps. Obviously if a watertight vessel is to be made the walls must be even, without cracks or holes, and the best way of achieving this is to press down each ring of clay onto its neighbour until it becomes oval in cross-section. Then, after every four or five rings, one must join up the coils on both sides of the pot with downwards pressure from the fingers or a tool. The photographs make this clear. When an enclosed shape is made, it is difficult to smooth over the coils on the inside, but one side at least

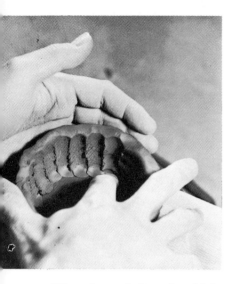

When the pot is four rings high, join the coils together with downward pressure from a finger on the inside, as shown above.

must be treated in the way illustrated. The fingermarks or tool marks are like throwing lines, personal to the potter, and an enormous variety of surfaces is possible. Some beginners leave—indeed are encouraged to leave—the coils on the outside untouched, so that the pot looks like a clumsy sort of Michelin man, in the mistaken belief that this is a more traditional or generic form. I have never seen a pot made in this way look other than ridiculous, and it is naturally weaker in structure if the coils are not joined up.

Many beginners, unable to grasp the principle of widening the pot's shape by adding ever-larger rings of clay, are paralysed into making a pot of continuous diameter, like a wobbly umbrella stand or an elephant's leg. Others over-ambitiously widen the pot which responds quickly by sagging out of shape or collapsing suddenly because of its unsupported weight. Pots started on small bases often appear to get wider and wider but no higher as each coil in turn spreads outwards, sags down and adds to the diameter of the base. Thus are ugly hyacinth bowls made, annually, by the thousand.

In making wide coil pots, anticipating collapse is essential. If the wall begins to bulge slightly, or the top appears flaccid or lifeless, then the next step is to put the pot into shape around its rim, and store it safely away on a shelf to dry. Depending on temperature and humidity, the pot will stiffen up in between half an hour and two hours, and work can then begin again. If the top coil becomes as hard as cardboard, it should be softened with water from a sponge run around the rim. Avoid using slip, which always makes everything sticky, and use water very sparingly, as it will run down the walls and can do damage to the base of the pot.

The outward curve of a coil pot can be reversed simply by using progressively smaller rings of clay. The problem of collapse is aggravated slightly in the early stages of narrowing, for the pressure

Join the coils on the outside too, taking care not to distort the shape with too much pressure.

This picture shows a rubber kidney being used to smooth the coils on the inside of the pot while the left hand supports the shape.

essential to join up the coils will be partly downwards, and as the top of the pot gets smaller it is progressively harder to get a hand inside to give the necessary support. Sometimes it is a good idea to fill the pot with crumpled newspaper, which has a supportive springiness and will, of course, burn away in the kiln. Other supports introduced in the making stage, such as props of clay, have a habit of getting jammed inside the pot, and if such a pot is fired it will rattle irritatingly for ever. The use of props on the outside to support a generously bellying form while it dries causes no problem; these can be removed later. The potter should take care to use clay which is slightly harder than the working clay for these props so that they do not stick permanently to the pot.

A fat ring of clay, like an inflated inner tube, arranged around the pot will help to support it while it is being widened. If a really shallow enclosed form is planned the walls can be permanently supported and strengthened inside with vertical ribs, like the balsa-wood fins which separate the membranes of a model aeroplane's wings. A shallow hand-built shape can be successfully supported in

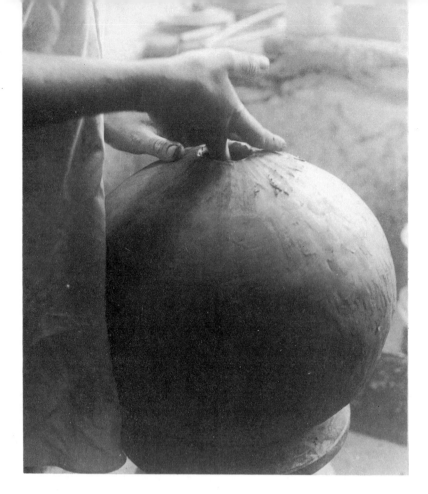

a plaster mould, and many fine modern pots have been made in this way. The shape of the lower part of the pot is dictated, however, by the mould and it is best to make a mould specially for the pot (see Chapter 11). A shallower curving base can be achieved by making the first few coils over a football, inverting the shape when it has dried a little. Such a shape would need a coiled footring for stability.

It is quite difficult to get a pot stable about its centre when coiling. The problem does not arise in throwing, and may take the coil potter by surprise. The pots on page 68 by Ruth Duckworth show her magnificent sense of balance in creating assymetrical shapes which do not fall over. Unstable pots usually have a short life and it is not wise to make wide coiled pots with too small a base.

Finishing the top of a coiled pot demands the same care as the top of a thrown form. It should be emphasised, and a roll of clay, perhaps of smaller diameter, can be added to the top coil to give it extra width. The pot in the photographs opposite has a top made from a coil of double the normal thickness. A constant-thickness wall is desirable for the rest of the form, and it certainly must not be thin near the base. Coil pots can afford to be heavier in relation to their size than thrown pots, and a coil pot which feels uncomfortably light in the hand is a poor specimen. Making coil pots with walls which are pathetically thin is one of two major mistakes made by the beginner; the other is starting the pot without the

Below: coiled Inca drinking vessel from near Pangoa in Peru.

faintest idea of what shape one wants to make. It is essential to start the pot with a clear idea of its finished form. It is a good thing to draw this on the bench top in pencil so that it is constantly before you. Although the finished result may not look like the drawing it will certainly be better than one made haphazardly without a preconceived form in mind, for in coiling, a good shape never comes about by accident. In the main the same general criticism of forms applies to coil pots as to thrown pots, with changes of angle (i.e. shoulders, flanges) attracting the eye and often indicating strength. Very rounded organic curves, and forms which squat low to the surface on which they stand are often peculiarly appropriate to coiled pots, and not to other techniques.

Once the coils are joined together, the surface can be left alone or, as with thrown pots, it can be treated as it grows harder and drier. Of all the tools I have ever used, an old hacksaw blade is the best I know for working the surface of a coil pot. Because it is flexible it can cope with changes of curve, as can a plastic comb. A smooth

The rough texture of this pot is made with a comb, and its top is smooth for contrast.

73

piece of wood used to beat the surface may also be useful and the beginner is invited to experiment. The texture left by fingers alone is not always very pretty but neither is a surface which is overworked. Impressed designs made with seals or stamps are not as effective as designs in applied relief, such as fins or ribs, and sometimes projecting lugs or handles added to a coiled pot become an integral part of its form.

Coiled pots tend to take longer than thrown pots to dry out because of their extra thickness. Occasionally the base of a coil pot will crack if it has become stuck to the surface on which it stands, and it is therefore important to make sure that the pot stands free on its bat or base before putting it away.

I suppose that pottery classrooms are littered with more bad coil pots than any other kind, usually broken and unfired. These spectres decorating the stage, and a general sense of purposelessness about the slow act of making a pot (whilst pots made on the wheel, however bad, seem self-justifying) must turn most beginners off coiled pottery for ever, if not ceramics as a whole. A wheel is not needed in order to make good pots, but care and concentration are. A bonus for those who persevere and an attraction for all is that coiled pots can be made big, very big. It is worth checking on the size of the kiln before you start.

Pottery made from thick coils can be treated sculpturally, like this incised 'coral' by Deirdre Bowles.

9 Hand made pottery:

Slab & pinched pots

Slab pottery does not mean what it appears to mean. It is neither flat nor undecorated. It is the technique of making pots out of sheets of clay rolled out like pastry, often using a kitchen rolling pin. The technique taught to beginners is often illustrated with examples of dreary shallow boxes filled with cactus plants, or dishes shaped like hearts, to show that the sheets of clay can be curved. Any technique can be used to produce something boring or ugly, but pots made from sheets of clay can be exhilarating and lively, and with its sculptural possibilities it is in this area of ceramics that one of the major growth points has been in recent years.

It is not a 'natural' technique in the way in which coiling and

throwing are natural developments to answer the need for practical vessels. Slabs of clay are not even as strong as pastry, but if they are handled when in exactly the right state of hardness, they can be most obedient materials. A rolled-out slab of clay is essentially a flat surface and, therefore, like a plate, a splendid vehicle for decoration, whether incised, embossed or painted. At the same time sheets of clay are pliant and can be folded like leather, though unlike leather they have no resilience to make them spring back again. The photograph on page 75 shows a ceramic form made entirely of folded sheets of clay, and demonstrates how slab-made ceramics can easily become sculpture. Whilst a pot made on the wheel is essentially abstract as it does not represent anything in nature, the

Rolling out and cutting slabs.

**Ceramic houses
by Bryan Newman**

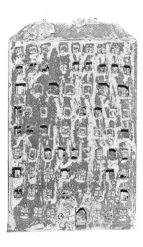

coiled hand-built pot can be made representational if desired, and sheets of clay combine a peculiar self-effacing anonymity with an essential clayeyness, so that each 'House' by Bryan Newman is both a house and a ceramic form at the same time.

The degree of precision achieved in throwing and turning is difficult to match with slab pottery, but the beginner is strongly advised to aim at a high standard of finish, and particularly at uniformity in thickness of slabs. Compared to the jointing of wood, slab building lacks all the sophistication of carpentry. It depends on butting clay together, and gluing simply with clay or water. Because the technique is so very basic the joins must be well made. Unlike coiled pots, where construction is masked by textures, slab junctions are often left bare and there is no excuse for poor workmanship.

The basic geometric shape in the picture sequence illustrates most of the problems encountered in making a slab pot. Wedged clay should be rolled out on a surface to which it will not stick itself, and the best insurance against sticking is to spread a layer of grog underneath the clay, like flour under pastry. The grog can be as fine as flour or coarse like sand, but in each case it will cling to the surface and if a grogged surface is not desired then rolling the clay out on a sheet of newspaper is best. The clay will stick to this, but it can be pulled off when dry. The advantage of rolling out the clay on a piece of heavy-weight canvas is that the clay sheets can easily be moved without damage by lifting the canvas. The clay, however, takes up the uniform texture of the canvas and this is not always desirable. Two flat pieces of wood of equal thickness placed on each side of the clay will restrain the rolling pin and the slab of clay so rolled will be of even thickness all over. An alternative method of making the sheets of clay is to pull a wire through a lump of prepared clay, raising the height of the wire by regular steps. The tool for doing this is shown in the picture below, and although it must

**Notched sticks and a wire allow
the potter quickly to make slabs
of predictable thickness.**

Separate the slices and when one has been cut to size use it as a template for its opposite number.

Using a modelling tool to improve the finish of the joints.

be carefully made it saves the slab-maker a great deal of time. The slices of clay, like slices of bread, should be spread out so that they are equally exposed to the air for drying.

The requirements for a pot of square plan with an open top are a base and four sides. The slabs should be allowed to dry a little before the squares are cut, and a clean, sharp, dry knife should be used. A plastic set-square will help to make the right angles at the corners and it is important to hold the knife vertically or the slab will have chamfered edges. The clay is pulled slightly by the knife and special care is needed, as when sawing through a plank of wood, towards the end of the cut. A slight distortion of the form at the corners can be corrected with the fingers, but it is best avoided in the first place.

When assembling, the sides can either be stood on the base or can lap around it. In the both cases an allowance must be made for the thickness of the clay. By lapping the sides in a follow-my-leader pattern, sides of equal width can result in a square plan, even when the thickness of the wall is taken into account. Like thrown pots, a slab box looks better if the line of its base is raised very slightly above table level, and if the sides of the box are thus fixed, slightly above base level, the box will look crisper and more alive. The technique of joining sides is similar to that of adding handles. The surfaces to be joined must be scored with a pin or knife (a cross-hatched pattern is effective) and a little water or slip added to fill up these score-marks before the two pieces are brought together. If a vertical wall is required it is a good idea to have a heavy, smooth and

Stages in the assembly of a slab pot. Before starting, the slabs should be dry enough to support themselves. Below: the base, by projecting below the walls, helps to 'lift' the pot like a foot.

Above: slab pots by Ian Auld

Below: rounding the inside corners

reliably vertical object like a brick handy so that the box can be rested against it to avoid collapse. Set up the walls one by one and use a wooden modelling tool to clean up the joints on the outside. A very fine roll of clay, about the thickness of a shoelace, can be added to the inside of each join and smoothed with a finger. This will give curved corners internally, much better for cleaning, without impairing the crisp right angles of the outside. The cube can be given a fixed top as well, glued to the walls by the same method. It is important to note that any form of this kind will seal air inside it, and the whole lot will blow up in the kiln unless a small air hole is made in the pot somewhere, preferably in the base. This hole should be not less than $\frac{1}{16}$ inch (2 mm) in diameter.

A top will have to take into account the thickness of the walls in order to be a perfect fit, and if it is to be a separate lid, it will need an additional wall on its underside to ensure that it grips firmly, like the throat of a thrown lid.

Allowing for the wall thickness in preparing slabs often confuses the beginner. If the follow-my-leader sequence is not adopted, a rectangular plan will result from the use of identical slabs, as the illustration below shows, and this of course may be the intention. Hexagonal, pentagonal and other plans can be made with slabs, as can irregular figures with many sides of different lengths. The joints will cease to be at right angles, but it is easier to cut the slabs with square edges first rather than angled ones, and to pare them to the correct angle at the time of assembly. It is often important to preserve the pot's hard edges, for aesthetic reasons, when it has dried. Sandpaper has a disastrous softening effect on the shape, and although you may want to use fine sandpaper on the sides of the pot, try to stop it blurring the edges. The walls of a slab pot can be given a decorative texture if the clay is rolled out over a patterned base. Old dishcloths, coconut matting, a scrubbed table top, even a

Identical sides will only make a square pot if the follow-my-leader sequence is adopted. Identical sides can make a rectangular plan if the arrangement far right is followed.

Crumpled slabs to make sculptural forms.

Stoneware chest of drawers by Ian Godfrey, made from slabs carved and decorated when leather hard.

grid cover in the road, provide good surfaces to experiment with (see page 130). Surface detail need not, however, be all over the pot and the plane surfaces of slab pots are well suited to applied and incised designs. Often a ridge of clay prepared in the same way as the slabs, fixed around the top of the pot or breaking up the elevation in a horizontal band will improve the basic slab form. The slab technique is appropriate for ceramic sculpture, and the range of possibilities widens if one considers using the slabs as curved forms. Caught at the right time clay can be persuaded to some extent into three-dimensional curves. Slabs which are curving, stretching, crumpling or breaking can be arrested in the act if the clay is supported while the slab dries. On page 86 are some simple sculptural forms which can be made, taking into account the clay's pliability. The slab technique is often more appropriate than coiling for pots which are oval in plan, and the opportunities for curved and interlocking shapes are endless.

Making a slab pot takes time and a lot of space in a crowded classroom. It also uses more clay than one expects. Clay for all the slabs must come from the same source, and preferably at the same time, as variations in clay may cause the pot to open up at the seams when it is being fired. Cutting squares or rectangles from a slab rolled out with a rolling pin leaves much unused clay round the edges, though this can be re-worked and re-used immediately, before it dries, in narrow strips for decoration or lumped together and re-rolled out to make additional slabs.

The slab method is sometimes combined with other techniques, and a composite pot made partly from slabs, partly from thrown pieces. The results of such a mixture can be unattractive, though there is no inherent evil in combining techniques. One's own aesthetic sense is probably the best guide and it is a sense continually called upon by the potter undertaking slab forms. Thrown and even coiled pots make themselves to a certain extent. Never so slab pots, where the potter is master and the clay is completely passive. If you can muster up good judgement and inventiveness you will be amply rewarded. The technique of rolling out and cutting shapes from clay extends from ginger-bread men and toys to the severe Oriental ceramics representing houses, groups of buildings and farms, and finely articulated units which fit together to perform a function or just to delight the eye and hand.

Right: pinched pots by Ruth Duckworth. Below: bashed pots with thrown tops.

Pinching and bashing

'Take a ball of clay and, with your fingers and thumb, shape it into a pot . . .' As easy as that. This humiliating exercise is often given to beginners in order to familiarise them with the material, and they soon find the ugly ball cracking and tearing, and rolling helplessly on its side. At best, a beginner may hope to produce something resembling a coconut shell, though if the walls are as thin as a coconut shell it will almost certainly break before firing, for unfired clay is very fragile. The art of pinching a pot—making a pot entirely from a single piece of clay by hollowing it out—demands experience, or even a tradition, and is best shown by the ceremonial tea bowls of Japan where the form, though thick in the wall, is studied to perfection. The rim, the profile, the base, the texture of the outside and the 'feel' of the finished pot in the hand can all contribute to the beauty of the whole. Concentration and sensitivity are essential if you are to make a pinched pot which is beautiful. A

83

**Pinched porcelain
by Mary Rogers.**

great deal of bogus nonsense surrounds the so-called qualities of lumpish shapes. Compare your work objectively with a Christmas pudding or a potato. Like other hand-made forms pinched pots can be magnificent, and some materials like porcelain body lend themselves well to delicate forms, but do not make pinched pots unless you can concentrate on them, and unless you really want to.

It is rather easier to bash or beat a piece of clay into an interesting shape, using a piece of wood or metal, though the achievement may not be much of a pot. If a lump of clay is fixed around the end of a piece of wooden battening (say 1 × 2 inches or 2.5 × 5 cm) dusted with French chalk and this is then beaten carefully on a flat surface, a form with flat sides can be produced. The best way of describing the technique is to imagine that you are trying to turn a toffee apple into a lump of sugar, without touching it by hand. These two techniques, which are capable of producing excellent pots, are so simple that one cannot describe them at length. To do them full justice, one must first dispel the mistaken impression that pinching and bashing clay is some sort of anguished act of a potter in despair. One should also banish the idea that this is a useful method of filling the last ten minutes of an evening class. The more thought and time given to the pots the better they are likely to be, and work by Mary Rogers in porcelain (above) illustrates how fantastic can be the result.

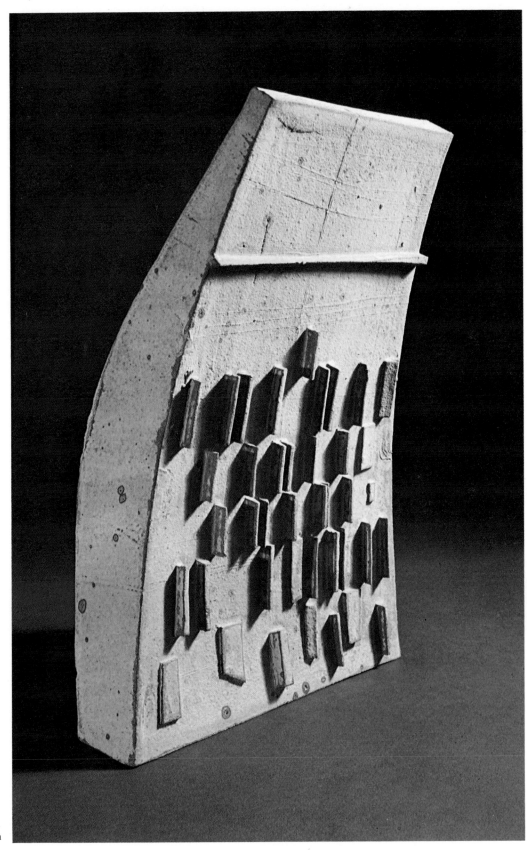

Slab form by
Bryan Newman

Slab forms b
the author

10 Mechanical aids for the modern potter

Up to this point, the pots and techniques described have involved the use of metal tools and only one mechanical aid—the wheel. If this assists the potter to tame centrifugal force and to create hollow shapes with a circular cross-section, then other machines can assist the potter to other ends.

A die stamper, which uses pressure to squeeze plastic material into a predetermined shape, can be used in pottery. If two hinged dies are squeezed together by hand a predetermined shape in the clay will be made, but it will be a solid rather than a hollow form. Such a device—which resembles a modern toasted-sandwich maker—can be made in metal or in wood, and has a respectable history dating back to Roman times when terracotta lamps were made in this way. It is swift, but only suitable for certain forms. Any studio potter designing a hinged press mould of this kind must choose the shape carefully. Undercut edges will not work successfully, and uninteresting shapes become very tedious when repeated *ad nauseam* from this kind of mechanical mould.

The pressing and squeezing of clay into shape has been combined with the wheel in one of the ceramic industry's most important techniques—jigger and jolleying. This process allows pots to be made on the wheel entirely mechanically, and all exactly the same. Clay of a consistency harder than would be used for throwing is laid over a mould fixed to the wheel head, and then pressed and scraped into shape by the lowering of a metal profile on an arm. This tool—the 'jigger'—when held against the revolving clay makes

The jigger and the jolley: metal profiles which are used to shape the clay on a wheel.

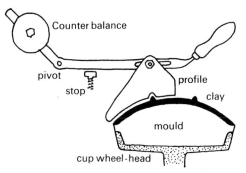
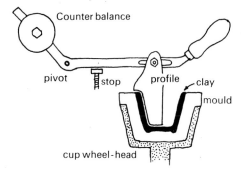

pots much as the woodworker's lathe makes bowls or chair legs. It is a useful but rather an insensitive tool, not much used by studio potters. The shaping arm can be used to form the *inside* profile of the pot, in which case the clay is cradled in an iron cup or 'jolley'.

Another machine which is gaining popularity is the wall-mounted extruder, which allows the studio potter by pulling a lever to press clay through a die, as toothpaste is squeezed from a tube, or cream from an icing machine. By using a long handle, an enormous force can be exerted without a great deal of effort, and the results have applications in all forms of hand-made pottery. By changing the die at the bottom of the cylinder the cross-section of the extrusion can be modified—from a circle to a square, or even a star. There is no limit to the length of the extrusions, other than that imposed by the siting of the extruder itself—its height above the floor—and the amount of clay it contains. Extruded ropes two or three feet long are usually as much as the potter will want to handle, however, and it must be said that these are tempting to the coil potter as ready-made coils. Gordon Baldwin has for a long time made large coiled bowls of great beauty and precision, using extruded coils. The resulting bowls, as shown alongside, have an 'other wordly' quality far removed from the organic pots of Africa which use coils rolled from under the fingers. However, the 'untouched by human hand' quality of the extrusion can be turned to the advantage of the studio potter, who will find that the extruded form can be bent and coaxed into shapes which are tense and springy, and make all other clay forms seem flaccid by comparison. The potter can use this simple mechanical device to assist him to make forms like those made in metal in a forge, though with a great deal less physical effort.

By inserting into the centre of the die a shape held on a strong tripod called a spider (see illustration) the extruded form can be made

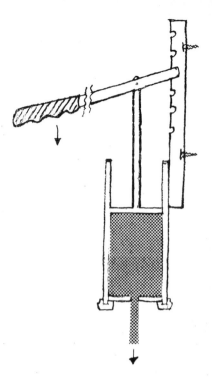

Clay is forced from a wall-mounted extruder by leverage. The extrusion will be solid, as shown below, or hollow, by means of the introduction of a 'spider', shown bottom left.

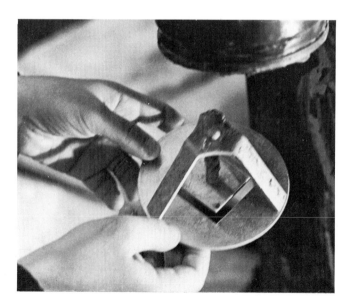

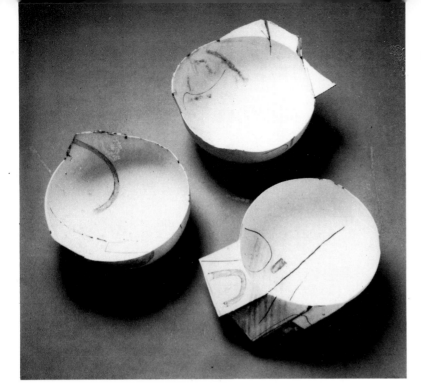

Left: three large bowls made by Gordon Baldwin from extruded coils. Below: sculptural ceramic by Anthony Hepburn using extruded sections.

hollow rather than solid. Thus tubes and quite intricate shapes can be produced. Manufacturers of hollow bricks use extruders and chop the sections up into manageable brick-sized pieces. Similarly a potter can experiment with clay extrusions, and by cutting them up into very short sections can use the pieces to assemble decorative sculptural panels which can be wall mounted or even used as room dividers, fired in sections and assembled.

By using fire clay in an extruder the studio potter can produce his own kiln furniture, and thereby save cost (see Chapter 18), but it is in the area of sculptural and decorative ceramics that this machine, designed for mundane purposes like producing drainpipes, has most application.

Tiles

Bricks and tiles are made mechanically, and while the studio potter is unlikely to want to make bricks, he may well want to produce tiles either for small panels or for more ambitious schemes. This is another form of ceramics in which a machine becomes a useful tool. Tiles are particularly susceptible to warping, a characteristic which is nearly always undesirable. To avoid warping, the thickness of the tile should be constant and its size must not be too large. Small-scale tiles, 2 × 2 inches (5 × 5 cm) for example, can easily be cut from a slab rolled out with a rolling pin. If the clay is at least $\frac{3}{8}$ inch (1 cm) thick, then warping will be minimal. These tiles made by hand can be used for chess boards if glazed in alternate contrasting colours.

Circular and hexagonal tiles are inclined to warp less than square ones, but are difficult to cut precisely by hand, and a tile cutter is

Making tiles with a tile cutter.

another basic machine which comes to the aid of the potter. It could hardly be simpler: it is a metal frame which is pressed into the clay, much as a pastry cutter cuts out crimped circles for jam tarts. The tile cutter, however, is assisted by a spring-loaded back plate, which will push the tile out as shown in the illustration, allowing the potter to produce tiles at high speed from rolled out slabs of clay. This is the only stage in tile making which is fast: the drying process must be extremely slow as a wet tile, left to its own devices, will curl up at the corners like an old sandwich. The potter has to keep his tiles in an atmosphere which is not too dry, and turn them over regularly as they become drier. They can be stacked in a staggered pattern, so that the weight is carried by the corners, keeping them down while air gets to the centres.

A regular, even surface is essential for some purposes—for example, where a tile panel is used for a large painted design. Many potters buy tiles ready made for such purposes and paint designs on top of the manufacturer's clear glaze (see Chapter 17). Floor tiles need to be fairly thick in order to withstand wear, at least $\frac{3}{4}$ inch (2 cm). Sometimes, however, the irregularities in a handmade tile can be quite appropriate. Tiles used for wall cladding are often given textures, or even carved relief. If visual impact and appeal is more important to the tile panel than practicability the potter should, nevertheless, remember the importance of ease of cleaning. Strong relief easily catches dust, and shiny glazed surfaces are simpler to wipe down than rough ones. The original use of tile cladding was part practical, part decorative, and the decoration often consists of a design greater than the unit dimension. The decoration of tiles is a subject on its own, and is discussed in Chapters 16 and 17.

11 Moulded pottery and slip casting

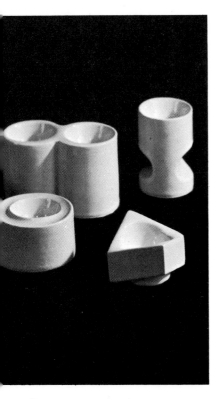

Slip cast egg cups by Melchior Wyt.

The third major category of pottery is that which is cast from moulds. In terms of quantity it is by far the commonest kind of ware, nearly all industrial pottery being made this way. For the studio potter and the beginner it is interesting and useful, but can be less directly creative and personal and it is a good deal less convenient in the small workshop than it is in a large factory. The possibility of being able to make identical units is important to anyone who wants to market a product, and in industry the relationship between manpower and output is impressive. One man with a can of casting slip can fill up a thousand moulds in a short time, but a thousand moulds take up a great deal of space, and in a small workshop casting does not compare with throwing for productivity. The act of the cast pot maker is the manufacture of a form in clay from a mould—a mould which may have been designed by someone else, perhaps even for another purpose. Moulds are usually made of Plaster of Paris, though fired pottery, wood or any absorbent non-deformable material will serve. The clay which is applied to this mould in industry is always in a very liquid form—as casting slip—though studio potters may work from plastic clay, rolled out as for slab pots.

Clay which has dried inside a mould must be capable of being removed without breaking, and thus complicated shapes such as teapots or even simple ones like china dogs are made from moulds which can be taken to pieces. Such moulds can be very complicated indeed, consisting of ten or more pieces, sometimes lining the inside as well as the outside of the form. Where the cast does not contain intricate shapes and undercut surfaces, the Plaster of Paris mould may be in one simple piece.

A problem for the slip caster is distortion of shape or breakage through shrinkage. The slip or liquid clay which takes on the form into which it is poured as a liquid must not shrink too much as it dries or it will naturally break apart. For this reason it has to be given very liquid characteristics with the minimum amount of water, and the ingredients or deflocculants which do this are sodium silicate, or water glass, and sodium carbonate or soda ash. The other ingredients of slip are ball clay, china clay, feldspar and flint,

Around a solid clay form clay
ramparts are built, strong enough
to hold in Plaster of Paris when
it is poured.

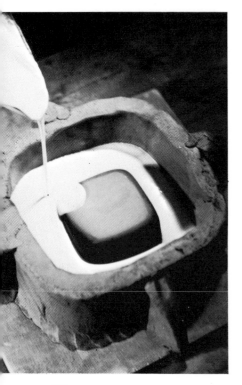

and a recipe for a casting slip will be found at the foot of the facing page, together with some instructions for its preparation and use.

The beginner who wishes to learn to cast will probably be offered someone else's one-piece mould to use, but if he has the initiative to make his own, he can do so in a single evening, in the following way. A solid form must be made from clay (or another plastic medium like Plasticine, if preferred) around which is poured liquid Plaster of Paris to make the mould or 'female' of the shape. The fine grainless plaster is going to reproduce mercilessly every flaw and irregularity of the potter's solid form, and once the mould is made it cannot be altered or cleaned up.

The form can be any shape in plan, but must not have undercut sides, and its casts are likely to distort if the dimensions greatly exceed 12 inches (30 cm). In the photograph the solid form is a rounded-off square, the shape of a television screen. It could be the shape of an oak leaf, in which case symmetry would be unimportant, but where the form is symmetrical, tools should be used to improve accuracy. The outline form should be drawn up on a piece of tough paper or card, and a symmetrical template should be used to check the accuracy of the shape (see drawing). If the template is made of perspex, hardboard or thin metal, it can be used as a scraper, helping to form the solid shape out of plastic clay as well as checking its profile. The clay used for the form should be a little bit harder than that used for throwing, and the surface can be improved for finishing by sprinkling with powdered grog or talc.

A rubber kidney, sponge or leather burnisher can be used, and the potter must not cease in his efforts until the form is smooth and 'true'. Of course, Plaster of Paris will reproduce the texture of roughened clay or any rough surface (art students never tire of casting their own hands and fingers), but it must be remembered that the clay cast will take up this textured surface only on the side which is in contact with the plaster, and the other surface may be made disagreeably and meaninglessly uneven.

When the form is ready, and in the centre of a smooth surface like a drawing board, a high and thick wall of clay should be built around it about 2 inches (5 cm) away from the edge of the form, and the height of the wall should be about 2 inches (5 cm) higher than the highest part of the solid. If this wall of clay has any sharp corners to turn, in going around the mould, they should be buttressed, as should any long straight lengths of wall.

Plaster of Paris is weighty, and extremely messy if it breaks through the wall and cascades on to the floor. Clay walls are better barriers against this sort of accident than adjustable wooden boxes made specially for the purpose, and should always be used, provided they are thick enough. The clay in the wall should be at least 1 inch (2.5 cm) thick, and should be firm but not too valuable as it is best thrown away after use, and not re-used.

The Plaster of Paris for the mould should be mixed in a single quantity, adding surgical quality plaster in a fine shower of powder

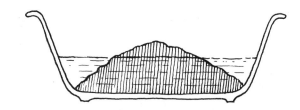

Plaster of Paris in a bowl of water, ready for mixing.

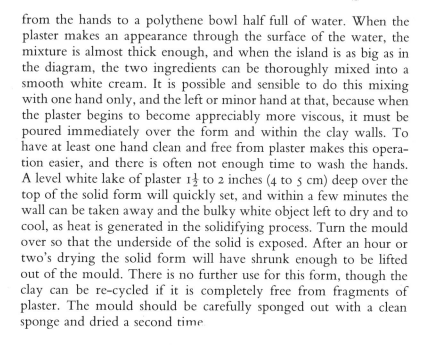

A template doubles as a scraper.

from the hands to a polythene bowl half full of water. When the plaster makes an appearance through the surface of the water, the mixture is almost thick enough, and when the island is as big as in the diagram, the two ingredients can be thoroughly mixed into a smooth white cream. It is possible and sensible to do this mixing with one hand only, and the left or minor hand at that, because when the plaster begins to become appreciably more viscous, it must be poured immediately over the form and within the clay walls. To have at least one hand clean and free from plaster makes this operation easier, and there is often not enough time to wash the hands. A level white lake of plaster $1\frac{1}{2}$ to 2 inches (4 to 5 cm) deep over the top of the solid form will quickly set, and within a few minutes the wall can be taken away and the bulky white object left to dry and to cool, as heat is generated in the solidifying process. Turn the mould over so that the underside of the solid is exposed. After an hour or two's drying the solid form will have shrunk enough to be lifted out of the mould. There is no further use for this form, though the clay can be re-cycled if it is completely free from fragments of plaster. The mould should be carefully sponged out with a clean sponge and dried a second time.

Casting slip

Porcelain is an increasingly popular material for studio potters. The casting slip recipe below makes a white, non-translucent porcelain which has to be fired to 1250°C.

ball clay	300 grams
china clay	2200 grams
feldspar (potash)	1250 grams
flint	1250 grams
sodium silicate	13 grams
sodium carbonate	13 grams
water	2.2 litres

The heavier the casting slip per litre of water, the better. This slip should weigh 1800 grams per litre—water on its own, of course, weighs 1000 grams per litre.

First mix together the two deflocculants, sodium silicate and sodium carbonate, and dissolve them in half a cupful of warm water. Add most of this to the measured quantity of water in the recipe, and then add this liquid to the dry materials. With your hands, patiently

Stirring porcelain slip will make it more liquid.

squeeze out all the lumps in the resulting gluey mass, and sieve through a 100-mesh phosphor-bronze sieve or lawn. Although the mixture appears to be far too gluey to be called a liquid, it is surprising how runny it becomes when stirred. Like a modern emulsion paint, it is a thixotropic gel.

Add more of the dissolved deflocculant to the slip when thinned, until the material will run off your fingers in long syrupy strands. It may not be necessary to add all the deflocculant you have mixed, but you must be wary of adding more than indicated in the recipe. Overloading the slip with these ingredients will cause it to change back from a liquid into an unmanageable jelly.

The production of this rather unearthly material is an interesting experience for any potter. When it has been allowed to mature for a day or two the slip can be used in single or multiple piece moulds. Multiple moulds for making, say, a coffee pot, are beyond the scope of this book but several books deal with the subject specifically, and the reader is referred to Dora Billington's *Technique of Pottery Making*, and the present author's *Pottery, A Modern Guide to the Art of Pottery Making* for step-by-step instructions. The following instructions indicate the use of casting slip in a single piece mould of the kind described on page 92.

The mould must be placed on a level surface, as the casting slip, smooth, even and creamy when it is poured in, must fill it completely to the rim without running over one of the sides. The absorbent plaster quickly soaks up moisture from the slip, and the level at the surface drops. More slip should be poured in to keep the

When surplus slip is poured out of the mould a 'skin' of clay is left clinging to the wall and forms the cast.

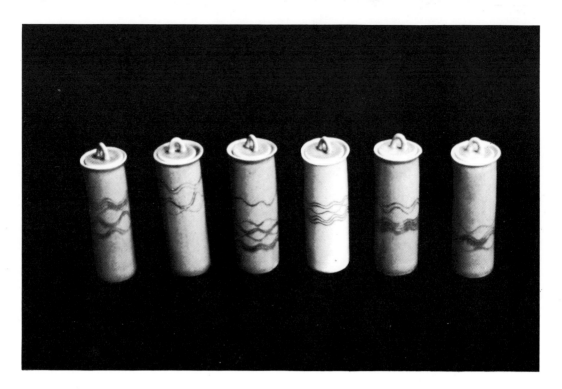

Slip cast porcelain jars by Gillian Lowndes.

mould 'topped up' and the topping up should be done gently, not from a height, in to the centre of the mould. If this is done roughly, the cast, when it emerges later, may carry scars or pock marks on its inside surface, caused by the arrival of the 'topping up' slip.

The vital and unanswerable question is, of course, how long does one leave the slip to harden against the sides of the mould. This depends on the degree of absorbency of the plaster, the amount of water in the slip and the desired thickness for the wall of the cast. Only the potter can establish all these, and he must choose for himself, but after a period of between ten minutes and half an hour he will be able to pour the slip off into a bucket or jug by tilting the mould, and will then see a residue clinging to the wall. Running a sharp blade or palette knife around the rim of the mould will remove the surplus slip dribbles and the rim is made straight and even. Experience will soon show how the blade should be angled acutely to the line of movement, so that the spare clay is lifted clear of the cast, and does not fall inside it to spoil the surface. As it dries it will leave the wall of the mould of its own accord, and at any stage from leather-hard to bone dry it can be tipped out. Needless to say, like any green pot, it is fragile at this stage and the thinner the wall or the more flat and open the shape, the more liable to breakage this new-born cast will be.

The optimum thickness of the cast will depend on the mood of the shape, but in general cast forms feel right in the hand if they are a little lighter and finer than thrown or hand-built forms. Slip-cast dishes are ideal subjects for decoration (see Chapters 16 and 17) but if this is to be applied as a slip before the first firing then the amateur potter might be wise to make this cast not from slip but from plastic clay which is more resistant in the green state.

Moulding

The technique of casting using sheets of clay is shown in the picture series. Plastic clay slabs will only form satisfactory casts if the angles within the mould are not too acute. A rubber kidney or sponge is useful to press the clay into any 'corners' in the mould, and where the clay emerges round the edge of the mould it must be cut carefully level with a sharp knife. A moulded dish can be decorated with slip (see page 134) whilst it is still wet and, like slip-cast dishes, lends itself to many different kinds of decoration as described in Chapters 16 and 17.

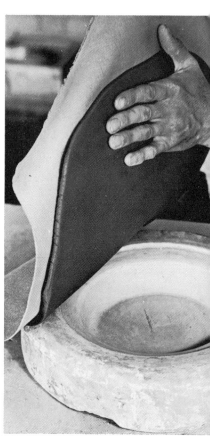

Roll out the clay on canvas, pick both up together and gently press the clay into the mould.

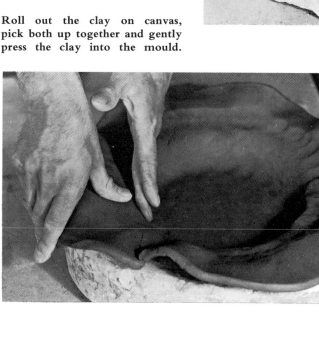

The quality of the inside of a shallow bowl depends on your skill in smoothing the surface with a tool such as a rubber kidney.

Rolled-out slabs of clay can also be used on convex Plaster of Paris or pottery moulds, known as 'hump' moulds. The slab is draped over the mould, trimmed and smoothed, and the results of this technique are equally appropriate for decoration. With hump moulds, the surface which is seen—the internal surface—is the one which has been in contact with the master shape, and this affects its character, which is more hard and neutral as a result. It is possible to use natural objects as hump moulds, and large sea-worn pebbles are very good for this purpose.

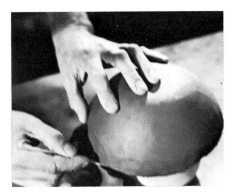

Placing, trimming and fettling clay on a hump mould.

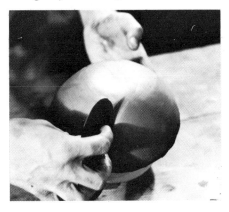

12 What's in a glaze

When a pot has been first, or biscuit, fired it is half made. The glaze, the style of glazing and decoration and the second firing complete the process, and there is a mating which is inseparable physically and aesthetically.

It is possible for a clumsy, lumpish biscuit pot to become beautiful if its glaze is a noble one, but more often a good biscuit pot becomes commonplace or downright ugly through poor glazing. The reasons can be many, including bad glazes, bad luck, an unpractised hand or just apathy. Potters of the world divide into two halves, the pot-makers and the pot-decorators, according to whether they are more interested in form or in surface, but those who primarily make pots for their shapes cannot afford to ignore the quality of the surface: glazes can play either a principal or a supportive role.

Glaze is glass, melted on to and then solidified on to the surface of a pot, providing a non-porous skin which increases the pot's life and makes it more hygienic and easier to clean. Like other forms of glass it is resistant to change and, however dirty or stained, can usually be cleaned without its own nature being altered. Though pots buried in the ground may gain a permanent patina from slow chemical attack, glazed ware approaches gold in its immutability once made. The earliest known glazed pots were made over 3,000 years ago, and are still sound.

Glaze and glass consist mainly of silica, which is also a major constituent of clay. By itself it has a high melting point (about 1,700°C) but is persuaded to melt at much lower temperatures when a 'fluxing agent' such as lead oxide, borax or sodium is present. The presence of alumina (aluminium oxide), also an ingredient of clay, with an even higher melting point, gives the mixture stability and adherence when it is in a molten state on the surface of the pottery.

Variations in the proportions of alumina, silica and the flux, and the influence of a whole host of other elements—titanium, calcium, potassium, zirconium, nickel and iron—are responsible for the difference in 'quality' of a glaze, i.e. its colour, texture, opacity, gloss and feel. Another factor is the method of application to the pot, and yet another, the thickness of the glaze layer, explained in Chapter 13.

The glaze ingredients, as finely ground solid matter, are mixed with water and applied as solids in suspension, the liquid conveniently disappearing into the porous surface of the biscuit pot, leaving the solid particles as a fine powder clinging to the outside. In this very vulnerable state the ware, with any painted or other decoration, is transferred to the kiln and refired so that the glaze melts.

For industrial purposes it is perfectly possible to grind up sheets of clear glass into a fine powder and spray this, mixed with water, on to ceramics, and cause it to reform on the pots as glaze. Industrial mass production, insisting on uniformity, requires chemists to make glazes, using the known characteristics of elements to alter and improve results, and calculating at a molecular level. Many beginners in pottery are frightened off by the thought of chemical formulae and molecular weights. This is unfortunate, as it is quite unnecessary to have any knowledge of chemistry in order to be a potter, and it is much more to the point to be a good cook. An analytical approach is more likely to be frustrating than fruitful at the studio pottery level, since the potter has little control over the precise chemical nature of his raw materials. Bernard Leach in *A Potter's Book* says, 'To a craftsman it is more important to know what works well than to know in precise detail why it works well.' Thus a knowledge of uses and effects of known materials is valuable to the glaze maker, and by experimenting he will come to know just what to add, and in what quantities, without the need to read a chemical formula.

There are, as explained in Chapter 1, two main types of ware, reflecting firing temperatures. For earthenware glazes maturing between 1,000° and 1,100°C, lead and borax are the commonest fluxes, and as raw lead is poisonous the studio potter knows it as lead 'frit', i.e. lead which has been combined with silica in a molten state, and ground to a non-toxic powder. Many schools and art departments now ban the use of lead in any form, and all earthenware glazes are based on borax, though lead frits are still readily available from ceramic suppliers, at high prices.

A colourless earthenware glaze, such as that described on page 119, is a basis for coloured decoration using metal oxides to add colour or to make the glaze opaque. Oxides can be bought in small and convenient quantities and are much more predictable in use than proprietary colours with names like 'salmon pink', and origins known only to the manufacturers.

Earthenware glazes are mainly shiny, the colours produced by oxides clear and even. Stoneware glazes are much closer in character to the clay, and in fact the glaze constituents are very similar indeed to the clay itself. The flux at stoneware temperatures of 1,250–1,300°C is either sodium or potassium, and the colour, which depends on all the ingredients of the glaze, is rarely clear and even. At high temperatures very small quantities of metal oxides in the clay body burn through the glaze making it spotty and blotchy, and colours are generally more muted and earthy.

Fortunately, natural raw materials like feldspar (a constituent of granite) contain the necessary flux, and potassium is, of course, also found in wood ash. As with earthenware, colourants are mainly oxides applied either in a pure state, ground down as powder, or in combined form as part of a natural material such as rutile, which contains titanium. Every glaze ingredient, however, must be applied as a finely ground solid, mixed with water.

The glazing room of an art school ceramics department or a large studio pottery is full of containers—small glass bottles containing apparently identical dark powders, and large bins or sacks holding yet more powders, mostly creamy-grey in colour. To the experienced potter, identification is easy—the glaze ingredients look and feel very different—but to the beginner it is something of a disappointment that there should be so much uniformity and drabness (it is sometimes hard to convince a beginner that a pale ginger-coloured liquid may produce a rich blue glaze). It is only in the kiln that the true colours and capacity of the oxides are revealed.

Exactly what glaze materials can do in combination with high temperatures is not just a lifetime's study, but a total preoccupation that binds together such unlikely groups of people as craftsmen, museum curators, industrialists and antique dealers. No book for the beginner should dwell too long on what is in a glaze but, based on my own experience, the following descriptions of the materials found in every glaze room may help the beginner to find what he wants.

Opacifiers

Tin oxide is traditionally the glaze ingredient for making opaque white. The tin in the glaze does not dissolve, but simply reflects light and masks the colour of the clay. Tin glaze is the white background of the enamelled or painted earthenware pottery known as majolica. Tin is effective as an opacifier up to stoneware temperatures, but is less used in high-fired ware as many of the raw ingredients of stoneware glazes, such as dolomite, themselves act as opacifiers. White tin oxide is an expensive material.

Zirconium is much used in place of tin oxide for white earthenware glazes. It is cheaper to buy, and has a more 'fluid' look after firing. In combination with colouring oxides it helps to make earthenware glazes bright and reflective.

Zinc Oxide is used particularly in stoneware glazes as an opacifier, as it tends to encourage crystallisation in the cooling glaze. It has a matting effect and 'crazes' if used in large quantities (see Chapter 15).

Titanium dioxide, well known as an opacifier in paints, tends to create a mottled effect when in combination with other oxides, by separating dark areas with tiny white speckles. On its own as an opacifier it is creamy in colour.

Opacifiers normally constitute less than 10 per cent of the total glaze ingredients.

Colourants

Iron oxide in one of its forms is the commonest colourant in ceramics. Known as ferrous oxide, ferric oxide, magnetite, ochre, haematite and crocus martis, or just plain rust, this brown powder, according to its strength, colours glazes from pale straw colour to dark treacly brown or black. In quantities around 6 per cent of the total glaze volume, it is characteristically ginger. In stoneware reduction (see Chapter 18) it helps to make the celadon pot green, grey or slatey blue in colour (see 5, page 104).

Cobalt oxide is the bright blue colourant familiar on 'Willow Plate', Meissen and many other designs. It is an expensive pigment, but very strong and so only small quantities are needed. It is often used in combination with other oxides which reduce its fierceness. Cobalt carbonate is similar, though a little cheaper, and less strong.

Copper oxide, like most colourants, is black in its powdered form, but a powerful peacock green when fired. As it is strong it is likely to go black if used in large quantities, and when used sparingly it is the pale green of oxidised copper roofs. In reduction stoneware (see Chapter 18) it changes completely to become the auburn colour of a copper saucepan. Copper carbonate is less strong in colour.

Manganese dioxide is a dull purple colour when on its own. Used with other oxides it softens harsh colours and particularly in combination with cobalt produces violet. At stoneware temperatures manganese dioxide has the useful property of acting as a flux, fusing on to a clay body without the help of a conventional glaze, thus making impervious vessels which are to be left unglazed. The picture on page 50 shows an example. It is also used as a clay body non-toxic form. As price and prejudice have increased, lead frits have become less common.

Nickel oxide, green in colour in its powder form, has a greying effect, ugly on its own but useful to soften harsh colours in high-temperature glazes.

Chromium oxide usually produces dull greens, though in combination with other oxides such as tin and iron it helps to produce pinks and yellows. I find it a nasty tiresome oxide which has often ruined glazes by bubbling, though some potters use it widely.

Vanadium, *antimony* and *uranium oxide* are useful in making yellow, especially in lead glazes. The last is rather hard to come by nowadays.

The density of colour given to a glaze by different oxides depends on their inherent strength, and the amount of oxide used. One per cent of iron would scarcely be noticed, whilst 1 per cent of cobalt would certainly show up as blue. When colouring oxides, alone or in combination, exceed 10 per cent of the total the glaze becomes unpleasantly metallic, uneven in surface and likely to have bubbles or 'craters' like the surface of the moon. Unevenness of surface is undesirable if the pot has to be used, and washed and dried, though uneven coloration is sometimes sought after. A mottled glaze may result from the inclusion of titanium dioxide or tin oxide with other colourants. A glaze will be spotty if the colouring oxides it contains are not finely ground. Most oxides are supplied already ground, but if they have coagulated into grains through moisture they can be ground again easily enough with pestle and mortar. When a randomly spotty glaze is wanted, it is best achieved by adding the colourant to the clay body, simply by sprinkling it into the plastic clay as a powder. The oxides will burn through the glazes as spots at stoneware temperatures.

To complete the tally of 'stock' materials in the glaze room, the following will be found in bins or sacks.

Lead bisilicate, lead sesquisilicate and proprietary lead frits, all fluxing ingredients for earthenware glazes, are combinations of lead, alumina and silica, fused and reground to produce a flux in a non-toxic form.

Calcined borax (sodium borate) is an alternative to lead as a flux for low-temperature glazes. Like the lead frits (above) this is a fine white powder.

Feldspar, probably in the largest sack, is the material used in most glazes as the source not only of alumina and silica but of sodium or potassium (according to its crystalline form), which act as a flux for high-temperature glazes. Feldspar all on its own will make a glaze at approximately 1,260°C, but not a very exciting one.

China clay (kaolin) ought to be pure alumina and silica, and nothing else, but most commercially sold china clays have trace elements which have marginal effects on the material, which is mainly used in high-temperature glazes. Alone, it refuses to melt. It is, of course, a key ingredient in casting slips (see Chapter 11 page 93). Light in weight and creamy in colour, it has a distinctive feel which a potter can recognise blindfold.

Ball clay is greyer than china clay when raw, and contains a larger proportion of trace elements. Important in clay bodies and casting slips, its use in glazes is mainly for high temperature ware.

Cornish stone, or china stone, is an alternative source of both sodium and potassium as a flux for stoneware glazes. It is used therefore instead of feldspar and is traditionally stained a pale duck-egg blue in its raw state, for recognition purposes.

Dolomite contains calcium and magnesium, both of which promote mattness in stoneware glazes. Dolomite is also an opacifier which combines attractively with many colouring oxides.

Earthenware bowl from Persia, thirteenth century. The dark design is painted under a clear glaze.

Whiting, derived from limestone, has a high melting point on its own, and although it produces a glaze in combination with other materials it often gives a matt surface.

Flint and quartz are silica, ground from different sources. They are alternatives for addition to glazes needing stiffener or hardener (i.e. more silica) and because they do not melt when uncombined are much used as a placing powder or batwash for kiln shelves (see Chapter 18).

Nepheline syenite, very rich in sodium and potassium, is a powerful flux for use in low-temperature or 'soft' stoneware glazes.

Talc (French chalk) contains a high proportion of magnesium, like dolomite, and helps to make a matt surface in stoneware glazes. Trace elements such as iron and titanium usually give a glaze containing talc a creamy colour when fired.

It is quite likely that a final bin will simply be labelled *Ash* and will hold the residual material from a bonfire. This 'potash', a rich source of potassium, has such a complex and varied chemistry that it has led many would-be analysts on long wild-goose chases in search of a scientific basis for its special qualities. It is a flux which gives colour, texture and surface of enormous variety, and it also has a lot of personality, which endears it to some potters and infuriates others. Working with ash glazes is much more like cooking than chemistry, and so a description of its collection and preparation is left to Chapter 14 on recipes.

Stoneware glaze tests: all the glaze tests on the left-hand side of the picture were fired to 1,280°C and all but the top one (Dark Green) came from a reduction firing in a gas kiln. The glazes on the right of the page were all fired to 1,250°C in an electric kiln, and the plainer, more even surfaces are typical of an oxidised electric firing. Recipes for the glazes can be found from pages 120 to 123, numbered as below.

Left side, top to bottom: 1. Dark Green *Body:* ⅓ 'T' *Material,* ⅔ *Moira mixture.* **2. 50:50** *Body: Potclays' Farnham Pink.* **3. Cone 8** *Body: Potclays' Farnham Pink.* **4. Black to Rust** *Body: Potclays' Farnham Pink.* **5. Queen's Celadon** *Body: Potclay's Farnham Pink.* **6. Red Reserve** *Body: Potclays' Farnham Pink.* **7. Velvet Mottle** *Body:* ⅓ 'T' *Material,* ⅔ *Moira mixture.*

Right side, top to bottom: 8. Abrey Crackle *Body: Potclays' Farnham Pink.* **9. 50:50. As No. 2 but in oxidised firing and more thickly and evenly applied. 10. Chessman Blue** *Body:* ⅓ 'T' *Material,* ⅔ *Moira mixture.* **11. BNO** *Body:* ⅓ 'T' *Material,* ⅔ *Moira mixture.* **12. Harriet's Brown** *Body: Potclays' Farnham Pink.* **13. Oak Ash** *Body:* ⅓ 'T' *Material,* ⅔ *Moira mixture.* **14. Gill's White** *Body: Potclays' Farnham Pink.*

13 Dipping and pouring and making a glaze

It is important to get the glaze on to the pot in a smooth and even layer, and this cannot be done with a paint brush. Spraying with some form of atomizer like a compressed-air spray-gun is an efficient and economical method for industrial purposes, but is unsatisfactory for the studio potter. Carefully timed bursts of spray directed at a revolving pot can give an even surface, but in the small studio there is a great deal of waste, for the spray which misses the pot cannot be gathered and recycled, and as hand-held sprays cope badly with concave or intricate surfaces, the studio potter is best advised to forget them.

Immersion in the glaze is the best method of ensuring an even coat, and the techniques to learn are *dipping* and *pouring*. The beginner will meet the glaze as a liquid of creamy texture made up from the ingredients mentioned in the previous chapter, and probably kept in a bucket with a lid. The first thing to do is to sieve the glaze, as its various ingredients have different weights and will probably have separated out into layers in the bucket. The most important ones, such as lead frit in earthenware glazes, go persistently to the bottom of the bucket, and every bit of glaze must be transferred through the sieve into another bucket to give a perfect mix again. A phosphor-bronze sieve or 'lawn' with resilient, fine and untarnishable mesh (of 100 strands per inch) in a wooden or plastic frame is needed for this, together with a scrubbing brush to help to push the stickier parts of the glaze through the sieve. The abrasive surface of the phosphor-bronze mesh makes short work of rubber gloves and quickly wears through finger nails, so the scrubbing brush and lawn should be regarded as inseparable, like a pestle and mortar. Both must be kept scrupulously clean, as specks of strong colourants like cobalt oxide left in the lawn or brush will show up in the next glaze which is sieved through it.

The act of glazing a pot appears simple and neat when done by an accomplished potter, but beginners find it a rather trying experience, and will learn faster if they have plenty of space on the bench in front of them, and plenty of glaze in the right shape of vessel. A bucket is a handy shape in which to catch the glaze after sieving, since an 8 inch (17.5 cm) lawn will usually fit comfortably

Sieving a glaze

in the top of it, and it is useful to have a jug handy and an enamel or plastic bowl of the size of a washing-up bowl.

Both inside and outside of the pot have to be covered with glaze, and the inside is normally glazed first. The jug should be filled from the bucket of glaze by pouring from the bucket into the jug (most beginners want to fill the jug by dipping it into the glaze, and if they do they will probably contaminate the glaze with whatever is on the foot of the jug). If the pot for glazing is cylindrical, glaze should be poured in up to the top, and then immediately poured out again into the plastic bowl which is conveniently waiting, empty, alongside. A quick rotating twist with the wrist as the liquid leaves the pot will shake off any droplets that would otherwise form on the rim. If any glaze runs on to the outside surface during this process it should be wiped away with a dry sponge, so that a double layer is avoided when the outside comes to be glazed. A biscuit pot will absorb the moisture from the glaze in a matter of seconds, and the glaze will be left dry on the surface.

The outside of a cylinder can most easily be glazed by inverting the pot, holding its base with the fingertips, and plunging it up the fingertips in the glaze in the bucket, holding it there for about a second before removing it. The air-lock, as in a diving-bell, will prevent the glaze from coating the inside a second time. One of the most infuriating things to arise at this stage is the discovery that there is not enough glaze in the bucket for you to be able to immerse the pot completely. The pot must not touch the bottom of the bucket or its glazed rim will be damaged, so it is wise to check the depth of

Pour glaze into the biscuit pot and then tip it out again immediately, turning the pot as you do so, to make sure that all the inside is covered.

Hold the cylinder vertical when dipping it into the glaze. This gives a better airlock and prevents the inside from being overglazed.

glaze against the size of the pot before starting. Another twist of the wrist helps to shake off the surplus glaze again, and if the pot is turned upright in the hand the liquid on the rim will spread out evenly, rather than in lumps.

This sort of care may seem obsessive to a beginner, but he will quickly learn that glaze put on unevenly will show up clumsily after firing, and that flaws cannot be touched up. A certain amount of gentle 'fettling' of the glazed surface with the fingertips before the firing will improve matters by smoothing down rough edges

Stoneware pots usually have their bases left unglazed, shown right.

and filling up cracks, but if this is done roughly lumps of glaze scale off altogether, and replacing them is difficult.

Marks on the outside of a cylinder where the fingers have held the pot are difficult to avoid if the glaze is to go right to the base, and the earthenware pot, which has a glazed base, may do better to be poured as described below. A stoneware cylinder, which is not porous when fired, needs no glaze at the foot and the dipper's art is to grasp the pot firmly in the fingertips whilst keeping them within $\frac{1}{4}$ inch (6 mm) of the base. Fingermarks showing on a glazed pot are not the most ugly of flaws, but they do not suit all pots.

Once a glazed area is dry it can be handled lightly without causing damage, and a cylinder can be glazed on the outside completely if it is glazed head-first up to half its height and then, when dry, base-first until the glaze lines meet. If the junction is a neat one it will not show, but if the glazes overlap there will be a change in glaze quality. Using two different glazes, of course, causes a decorative effect where they overlap, and this is described in Chapter 17.

The glazing of a large open form like a bowl demands more skill than a cylinder. Since the circumference of the rim is large relative to the rest of the pot, the glaze poured into the inside has a long way to travel as it is poured out again if the whole surface is to be covered. The hand holding the bowl must be conveniently placed to allow the potter to twist the pot through almost a complete revolution as he pours the glaze out again. Too much hesitation in pouring out the excess may mean too thick a coat of glaze, and pooling in the bottom of the bowl when the glaze melts.

Beginners are inclined to rush this stage, pouring out the glaze too quickly and leaving large areas of naked pot. If this happens, more glaze should be poured in straight away from the jug—the resulting overlapping will probably show, but the only other alternative is to wash all the glaze off again with water, and begin again when the pot is dry, which takes a long time.

When the interior of the bowl is dry, it can be inverted on the fingertips and held like a mushroom, with the potter's arm as the stalk. Long fingernails will damage the interior glaze, but fingertips will not. The outside can be glazed in this position, the glaze being poured over the outside from a jug held in the other hand.

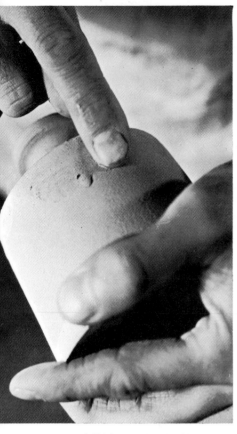

Some dribbles are inevitable, especially when one is learning. If they are left on they will probably show after the pot has been fired, but they can be removed by rubbing gently with the fingertip.

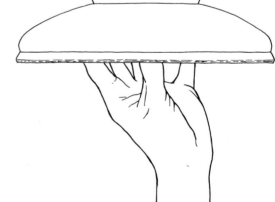

Far right: glazing the inside of a big bowl. To glaze the outside, small shallow bowls can be held on the fingertips; large deep bowls should be placed on battens (see overleaf).

The pouring of the outside of a really large bowl is best achieved by resting the bowl, inverted, on two thin strips of wood or metal (strong, long knitting needles will do) which lie across the rim of a plastic bowl. Glaze poured from a jug on to the outside will, if a steady rotation is followed with the jug hand, cover the naked surface of the pot without overlapping. The rim itself may probably benefit from a quick dip in the glaze when the outside is dry enough to be held by the foot, to cover up the marks left by the battens or knitting needles. It is a time for waterproof clothing, for beginners can expect to spill glaze over the bench, the floor and their shoes in the excitement of the moment. A useful aid saving much time is a banding wheel on which the plastic bowl, battens and inverted pot can all be rotated, giving the potter the chance to stand still while pouring glaze from the jug in his hand.

Small bowls and other open-shaped vessels can be glazed in one swift movement by immersing them completely but briefly in the glaze at an angle, holding them by the foot. A bowl so glazed should have a clean, even coat and an unblemished rim. The many shapes intermediate between cylinder and bowl all demand individual treatment, and it is often wise to suit the shape and size of the glaze bucket to the pot about to be glazed, especially when the glaze itself is limited in quantity. When trying to roll a pot in a saucerful of glaze it is as well to remember that a good glaze poorly applied is usually less satisfactory than an ordinary glaze put on perfectly.

Pots with handles, like jugs, are often a joy to glaze for with the handle immersed first up to its junction with the pot, the whole of the pot can then be held by the handle when this glaze has dried, and immersed, inside and outside being covered in one operation

Wooden battens can be used to support large or awkward shapes when glazing the outside.

Unblocking the holes in a tea-pot's spout after glazing.

with no fingermarks to spoil the surface. Teapots, on the other hand, are more tiresome than most to glaze because of their spouts. The pot's pouring capacity will be tested when the glaze flows for the first time down the spout, and the potter *must* remember, when all the glaze has gone, to unblock the holes in the base of the spout, or glaze will fuse across them and no tea will ever be poured. If the lid of the pot, which can be dipped on both sides into the glaze, is to be fired sitting in the pot, glaze must be wiped carefully off both the seating and the throat with a sponge, or the lid will never come off, and the teapot will be useless. An alternative method of keeping the join clear of glaze is to paint wax on to the seating before glazing (see Chapter 17).

A sponge can be helpful for cleaning glaze off areas where it is not wanted, though it should never be used, either wet of dry, to smooth down unevenly glazed areas as it will pull the glaze away from the pot. The paint brush, archetypal tool of the retoucher, is no use at all to the pottery glazer, for it will not apply glaze evenly and is as likely as the sponge to pull off what is already on.

By now the beginner must feel bewildered by the admonishments and advice, and unnerved to find that what should be a mere finishing stage appears to be the most difficult process of all. Hand glazing is quite difficult to do well, but it should be encouraging rather than the reverse that no tools are as good as one's own hands for applying and 'fettling' the glaze. Indeed, the best way to correct a minor flaw such as a chip of glaze which has fallen off the rim of a pot is to apply a droplet of glaze to the spot with the tip of a finger.

A smooth and even coat is essential for earthenware and a pot once glazed all over should be seated on a 'stilt'—shown in the drawing on page 150. The three points of this tripod leave only the finest marks on the base of the pot, and do not allow the pot to soak up moisture after firing. Once established on its tripod in a safe position, the pot should be handled as little as possible during any subsequent decoration, and put into the kiln for firing at the earliest opportunity.

Stoneware glazes vary more markedly in colour with the thickness of application than their earthenware equivalents, double layers showing up as lighter patches, but at the same time the streakiness of uneven application is not always a fault and the stoneware potter is rarely aiming to get a perfectly uniform coloration. The hand method of glazing is more appropriate to stoneware, and for beginners it is easier to learn dip and pour with stoneware glazes. Their ingredients have better adhesion to the surface of the pot when dry, and so they are less likely to get damaged on their way to the kiln.

It may come as a jolt to a beginner with his mind full of museum ceramics, or merely bent on completing a furnishing colour scheme, to be asked at an evening class, 'What glaze do you want, shiny blue or shiny transparent?' It is unfortunately rather common for evening classes to provide ready-made glazes of a very boring kind, and it is

not always popular to want to provide your own. The reason is that damage to the kiln and other pots can occur if a glaze is used which matures at a temperature lower than that to which the kiln is fired. Therefore the first step is to establish the firing temperature of the kiln, and to make sure that specially-made glazes fit this temperature.

Ready-prepared glazes can be bought from ceramic suppliers, but there is not much joy in using them, and glazes can be made so easily from a small range of materials that the beginner should be encouraged to try. The results, if not always perfect, will at least be as personal as the pots. Typical and useful recipes are given in the next chapter, and these are mixed simply by weighing out the ingredients and adding water. Glaze materials are supplied finely ground, though some of them are likely to go lumpy in their bags. It saves time and energy later if the lumps are crushed in a pestle and mortar or between the fingers before the materials are weighed.

I must confess that more than once I have started to make up a batch of glaze (6 lb or 3 kilo of dry materials is a sensible minimum quantity) only to find half way through that I have not had quite enough of a certain ingredient to complete the mixture. The result of being 'short' on one material can be interesting but it is more likely to make a disappointing glaze, so my advice is to assemble the materials in the sacks, bags or bins, and if one ingredient is low in quantity weigh that up first, and if necessary reduce the other ingredients proportionally.

There is no significance in the order in which dry materials are mixed, but the weights must be right, so ensure that the balance is clean and that your arithmetic is correct. Metric measures are useful when dealing with recipes in percentages but, equally, 100 oz of glaze can be made very quickly by weighing out the percentages as ounces.

Medium-hot water added to the ingredients will help to soften any remaining lumps, and to persuade the mixture to go through a lawn into another bowl or bucket. A 100 mesh lawn should be used and great care taken that all the ingredients go through, for if any stay behind in the bristles of the scrubbing brush, for example, the glaze mixture will be inaccurate. Two or three sievings back and forth from bowl to bowl may take up to half an hour, depending on the ingredients. Adding more water speeds the process, but if it makes the glaze too thin and watery it must be poured off later when the constituents have settled, and an over-thinned glaze cannot be used or tested immediately it has been made.

Mix the glaze ingredients with water and after sieving make sure that nothing is left in the lawn.

The perfect consistency of glaze is impossible to define, since it depends on the porosity of the pot and the optimum glaze thickness on the surface. Stoneware glazes, particularly those containing ash, are usually applied thicker than earthenware glazes, and to describe the consistency as 'like thin cream' is meaningless since cream varies as much as glaze. However, if it is as thin as milk, it is too dilute for use, and some of the water must be removed.

Once the consistency is right, the ingredients must be kept

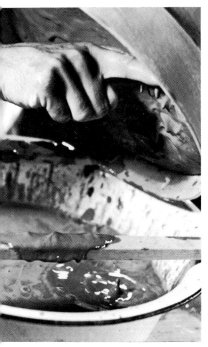

thoroughly mixed by regular stirring, or by the use of a glaze suspender. Some potters add bentonite up to 2–3 per cent by dry weight in place of china or ball clay, as this has the fortunate property of holding all the glaze ingredients in suspension.

The first thing to do with a new glaze is to test it. Most studio potters have favourite shapes of clay on which they make their tests, varying from small egg-cups to flat and indented tiles. An arch of thrown clay cut from a cylinder, as shown on page 104 is convenient since it will show the effect of concave and convex surfaces on the quality of the glaze, and also how the glaze behaves or 'breaks' on the edges.

It is wise to test a glaze on several clay bodies if more than one clay is used, since the glaze/body marriage is different in each case. Finally, it is vital to label the glaze test somewhere, by painting a number or a name on it in a metal oxide, which will stay legible after a firing. A glaze test is only any use if one knows what it is. The same applies to the liquid glaze of course, and glazes stored without names are a trial and a torment in almost every pottery studio or classroom. When one is in the middle of glazing, laying one's hands on an indelible writing instrument is hard, and the best thing to do is to tie a felt pen on a string to something immovable, like a water tap. Numbering the glaze bucket or jar is enough for identification, but if you can bring yourself to write the whole recipe on the label it may help others to save time in making up new batches.

I find that sweet jars with wide necks, which can still be bought cheaply for their replacement value from confectioners, are admirable for storage, and two of these will comfortably hold 100 oz of glaze, mixed with water. The great advantage of these jars is that one can get one's hand inside when necessary to prise out the sticky parts of the glaze which sink to the bottom when the jar has been standing for a while.

Glazes in jars or lidded buckets should last indefinitely, and so should plastic bowls and jugs. Phosphor-bronze lawns, however, which are expensive to replace, are soon ruined if they are left to soak in water, for their wooden frames swell and come unfastened at the sides. The fine mesh itself, though strong, can be punctured if heavy tools are left inside, and it only needs a small hole for it to become quite useless. This vital tool in the making of glazes should not be left in the sink, or flat on a shelf. It should be hung vertically on a short nail on the wall.

14 Recipes and results

A potter I know in Portugal makes unglazed earthenware, in the traditional amphora shape, for holding drinking water, kept cool by evaporation. His kiln is fired by solid fuel, mainly wood, but in the appropriate season he burns almond shells. Once every two or three minutes throughout the duration of this firing, shovelfuls of almond shells go into the fire-mouth, very black oily smoke comes from the chimney and the small mountain of almond shells, delivered by the lorry load, becomes imperceptibly smaller. The white ash which accumulates below the fire is of no use to him as a glaze flux, since he makes no glazed stoneware, but he gave me some to make a glaze test.

The collection of wood or vegetable matter ash to make a glaze has the faintest flavour of alchemy, mainly because the books which treat it in detail scorn to tell the beginner what to do with the ash when he has collected it, and just how to turn it into one of the bland grey powders which are mixed together for a glaze.

Potassium-rich wood ash is a flux or glaze-melter, and is combined with clay—alumina and silica—to make a stoneware glaze. The fascination for the beginner or amateur potter of ash glazes is that there are very few ingredients, and the wide variety of colours, textures and qualities come from the trace elements in the wood ash, so the potter, in collecting and preparing the ash, is truly participating in the creation of something unique. Because different kinds of ash and different batches vary enormously in what they contain, the ceramics industry, which needs to be able to repeat or sustain a colour indefinitely, is not interested in ash glazes. The studio potter therefore experiments alone, but fortunately no technical help is needed to develop and 'invent' a range of glazes.

The permutations of alumina-silica ingredients are wide, and experiments to see how ash from one source compares with another must stick to a standard recipe such as No. 13 on page 122 so that there is a 'control', and comparisons are valid. The variable is the ash, for different species of tree contain different trace elements in their wood, as do grasses and other vegetable matter. On top of this, the local soil conditions, which provide the chemicals for the tree in the first place, vary widely, so it is not possible to predict results with any accuracy. We only know that ash glazes extend from creamy white through greens and greys to bright orange, in both oxidised and reduced stoneware firings, (in an oxidized firing there is an adequate supply of air for combustion; in a reduced firing air flow is restricted. See Glossary).

All wood ash provides an appropriate flux, with the trace elements making the colour, but unfortunately the ash of other materials (such as coal) spoils the result, and it is essential to know that vegetable matter and nothing else has made the ash. Wood fires often contain a mixture of several woods, which does not in any way spoil the end glaze; it simply makes it impossible to get the same result again.

Anyone with a log-burning stove or fireplace is well placed to collect pure and controlled ash—simply by catching it on a foil sheet placed under the firebars—but the plight of the flat-dweller is not hopeless. Outdoor bonfires, the fires of wood scraps after tree-felling and even autumn fires of garden leaves yield perfect ash, provided that it is collected before rain has leached valuable chemicals out of it, and that no earth is scooped up with it. Since it takes an enormous amount of wood to produce sufficient ash to make even a small amount of glaze (1 lb or 500 grams of ash is a minimum working quantity) enthusiastic beginners are inclined to scoop up roots, sand and grit from the base of the fire in an attempt to get all of the ash, and thereby they waste the lot by including impurities. It is best to leave suspect ash behind, and to collect only the fine white or ochre coloured powder in a metal tin, preferably while it is still warm. There is nothing magical about this super-freshness; it simply ensures that everything in the ash is still there and that nothing has leached out or blown away.

Plunging all the ash in water in a polythene bucket immediately separates out the light, unwanted charcoal from the dense ash, and this charcoal, together with the grey scum that surrounds it, should be scooped off. At this stage the ash has to be treated with respect for, mixed with water, a fairly powerful alkali solution has been formed (caustic potash, or potassium hydroxide). If your hands or scrubbing brush are left in the liquid, they will begin to dissolve, and most potters know the characteristic soapy feeling of the fingers when they have been fishing pieces of charcoal out of the ash for a minute or so.

If the potassium in the ash is very concentrated the alkali can have quite spectacular effects. The almond shell ash my Portuguese friend gave to me quickly removed all the green paint from the metal bowl in which I soaked it, and did not stop there. Wanting to reduce its weight and size for transport by air back to England, I dried the stuff to the shape and texture of a damp brick, and wrapped it carefully in polythene bags, newspaper and a rush basket. In a few hours on the wooden shelves of the left luggage hall at Lisbon airport it had eaten its way through all this packing and was making a nasty mess on the shelf.

The taming of this ash had by now become a challenge, especially with the possibility of some truly unique colour or texture as the reward. Alas, when the ash was finally mixed according to the recipe on page 122, the result was one of the nastiest, oiliest, shiniest glazes I have ever seen, unpleasant to touch and heavily crazed. One of the lessons to be learned from this is that the greater the potassium content of the ash, the more powerful the flux in the glaze and the more 'glassy' the result is likely to be. Potters reduce the potassium content in the ash once it has been sieved in a very unscientific way by pouring it off as potassium hydroxide when the solid matter has settled. This process is known as 'washing', and could be said to require the intuition of a good cook. The more often water is added to the bucket of ash, and then poured off when the ash has settled, the more potassium is lost, though there is no easy way of measuring this. The resulting glaze will become 'harder' (i.e. will need a higher temperature to mature) and will probably become more matt with each potassium loss. This may lead to a more exciting glaze, or the reverse, and is certainly the reason why one potter's ash glaze will never be the same as another's. To pour away the potassium so prodigally may seem a waste, but feldspar as a second ingredient in the glaze also contains a flux, and the potter may only be interested in the colourants which are locked in the chemistry of the tree. No one can state precisely how much potassium hydroxide should be poured off an ash to get the best results, but if half a bucketful of dry ash is then filled to the top with water, half the liquid can be poured away when the ash has settled, the bucket filled up again, and the process repeated three or four times without harm.

The ash has to be turned back into a dry powder before it can be weighed against other dry ingredients such as feldspar, ball clay or china clay, so the clear liquid should be poured away carefully after the final 'wash', leaving the sediment behind. The sediment needs time to dry out, and the process of preparing an ash is spread over several weeks, especially if it is done at an evening class. Ash only appears in two of the glaze recipes which follow, but the small saga of collecting and preparing it is recommended to the beginner, and the results can be truly superb.

A most memorable experience in glazing was to make a batch of glaze from the ash from peat blocks from Sedgmoor in Somerset, burnt in one weekend in my own living room fireplace. The glaze test was a rich orange, with depth and a fine surface, and the subsequent pots were a joy. The source of peat blocks has gone, and the glaze cannot be made again. I only regret that there is not a drop left to include with the tests shown on page 104.

After such a long description of a single glaze ingredient, the reader may fear a similar treatment for all the others. There would be little point, however, as the studio potter or beginner is dependent on his supplier for these other materials, and they vary widely, though the supplier is quite likely to provide an analysis if requested. For those beginners who are encouraged by Chapter 13 to make their own glazes, I have included twenty-one glaze recipes which I have used and found satisfactory. Twelve of those suitable for stoneware are illustrated on page 104.

Because of variations in kilns and ingredients, it is unlikely that your results will be the same as mine, but they should certainly be interesting and will provide a basis for the home potter. The figures represent relative proportions. They can be ounces, grams or pounds, according to the quantities required.

Earthenware glazes
not illustrated

Honey Glaze   1,000°C
80 lead bisilicate
20 body clay

A clear to honey coloured glaze, the colour depending on the body clay, which should be the same as that used for the ware. Because of its low temperature, this glaze can be useful for home-made kilns with uncertain maximum temperature (see Chapter 18).

Transparent (opaque white) Glaze   1,060°C
56 lead bisilicate
30 feldspar
 7 china clay
 5 whiting
(10 tin oxide)

This is a useful transparent glaze, good on slips. With the addition of 10 parts tin oxide it is an opaque white majolica glaze.

Opaque Lead Glaze   1,030°C
35 lead carbonate
17 feldspar
20 flint
 8 whiting
12 china clay
 5 tin oxide

A low fired white glaze that is reasonably economical in the use of tin.

Leadless Glaze   1,140°C
12 calcined zinc oxide
56 feldspar
25 colemanite
10 barium carbonate
33 flint
 1.5 calcium nitrate

Many communally used potteries now prefer leadless glazes. This glaze matures at a temperature above normal earthenware, and is appropriate for certain body clays.

Matt Black Earthenware 1,060°C

64 lead bisilicate
21 china clay
 9.5 Cornish stone
 5 whiting
 4 manganese dioxide
 3 red iron oxide
 2.5 cobalt oxide

The high concentration of metal oxides makes this glaze susceptible to bubbling if it is applied too thickly.

Stoneware glazes

see page 104.

The numbers refer to the key to the photograph on page 104. The description 'reduced' or 'oxidised' relates to the examples shown in the photograph—all the glazes can be used in a reduction or oxidation firing, but the results will differ.

1 **Dark Green** oxidised 1,280°C

48 feldspar
22 china clay
20 whiting
10 flint
 3 copper oxide

A handsome dark green glaze with a very smooth surface and small black mottlings where the copper oxide shows its strength. An addition of 1 per cent cobalt oxide and 1 per cent tin oxide makes an equally rich dark blue.

2 and 9 **50:50** reduced/oxidised 1,250°C

50 wood ash
50 china clay

The china clay gives the opacity and dryness, the wood ash the colour. The surface is so dry that it is not suitable for table ware. When a nickel and cobalt mixture underlies this glaze it becomes blue-grey (see page 85).

3 **Cone 8** reduced 1,280°C

40 feldspar
30 quartz
20 whiting
10 china clay

A useful semi-transparent glaze, cold in colour when reduced, warmer in an oxidised firing. The speckles in the illustration come from the body.

4 Black to Rust   reduced 1,280°C

75 feldspar
15 whiting
5 china clay
5 flint
10 red iron oxide

This glaze produces dense glossy black where thick, changing to warm brown where thin.

5 Queen's Celadon   reduced 1,280°C

50 feldspar
50 whiting
40 ball clay
13 china clay
4 calcined ochre
3 red iron oxide

This celadon will 'pool' to a translucent green where it is thick. The colour becomes cooler with more complete reduction. Calcined ochre is an orange powder made from raw (yellow) ochre which has been heated until its colour changes. If raw yellow ochre is used instead, the surface will be less shiny.

6 Red Reserve   reduced 1,280°C

26 ball clay
26 quartz
21 feldspar
16 whiting
12 red iron oxide

A lustrous purple-red glaze. If titanium dioxide is painted on it has a golden sparkle.

7 Velvet Mottle   reduced 1,280°C

30 feldspar
24 china clay
16 whiting
12 flint
12 talc
6 ball clay

A very typical stoneware glaze, with an attractive smooth surface coloured on the photograph by speckles which have burned through from the body. It varies greatly in colour and quality according to the clay.

8 Abrey Crackle   oxidised 1,250°C

40 feldspar
30 whiting
25 stoneware body clay
25 ball clay
 5 titanium dioxide
 0.25 cobalt oxide
 0.25 nickel oxide

Crackle in the name does not mean crazing in the glaze but refers to the granular appearance which comes from the titanium dioxide. If the cobalt and nickel are reduced in quantity, or omitted, the texture remains and the colour pales.

9 See 2

10 Chessman Blue   oxidised 1,250°C

Ingredients as for BNO (11) with the addition of 5 per cent cobalt. The dolomite as an opacifier makes a muted purple when the glaze is applied thickly. It is not so attractive if the glaze coat is thin.

11 BNO   oxidised 1,250°C

50 Cornish stone
25 china clay
20 dolomite
10 quartz
 5 whiting

Matt surfaces sometimes look underfired. This one does not. Dolomite gives this glaze its characteristic quality and also softens and modifies the normally strong oxide colourants. An addition of 5 per cent iron oxide and $2\frac{1}{2}$ per cent tin oxide produces a waxy Indian red. Addition of 5 per cent cobalt produces the muted purple seen in recipe 10, called Chessman Blue.

12 Harriet's Brown   oxidised 1,280°C

46 feldspar
19 china clay
16 dolomite
11 flint
 3 red iron oxide
 2 copper carbonate

This glaze becomes glassy at cone 9 (1,280°C) but has a mature velvety surface at 1,250°C which is also attractive. When really thick, the glaze develops creamy areas, like cream on black coffee.

13 Oak Ash   oxidised 1,250°C

40 oak ash
40 feldspar
20 ball clay

A typical ash glaze, creamy coloured, with honey-coloured patches. Variations in colour, according to thickness, are characteristic of ash glazes. Other woods yield slightly different colours.

14 Gill's White   oxidised 1,250°C

- 50 feldspar
- 20 zinc oxide
- 10 whiting
- 10 tin oxide

A simple formula for a useful shiny white glaze, appropriate for the insides of stoneware pots. A little quartz may be needed to counteract crazing for the formula does not suit all bodies. It is excellent and less shiny as a glaze for once-fired ware. Like all glazes including tin oxide, it is expensive to make.

The following additional glazes are not illustrated in the colour plate, but are well worth trying.

Father's Matt Stoneware   1,250°C

- 30 whiting
- 28 feldspar
- 25 buff body
- 17 china clay

An alternative stoneware glaze which can be made blue with the addition of 2 per cent cobalt, brown/red with the addition of 12 per cent ferric oxide.

Celadon   reduced 1,250°C

- 48 feldspar
- 22 china clay
- 20 whiting
- 10 flint
- 2 ferric oxide
- 2 bone ash

This green glaze is included because it is very effective when used over a white slip comprising 50 per cent ball clay and 50 per cent china clay.

Porcelain Glaze   oxidised/reduced 1,250–1,280°C

- 40 feldspar
- 38 china clay
- 20 whiting
- 15–20 wood ash
- 0.1 copper oxide

A beautiful waxy glaze, very white on sharp porcelain edges. The copper oxide will make pale turquoise provided the constituents of the ash do not provide their own strong coloration. A normal hardwood ash will produce a glaze which is honey-coloured where thick.

Janet's Ironstone Glaze   reduced 1,250°C

50   ball clay
50   ground iron-bearing limestone
10   whiting

When reduced in an open muffle kiln, an olive green-to-gold runny glaze, magnificent on shallow bowls and platters, was the result of grinding up a particular limestone from Somerset. Obviously the subtle coloration depends on the trace elements in the stone. A stone pestle and mortar, or other equipment, is necessary for grinding soft limestone to fine powder. This interesting glaze is included to encourage enterprising potters to try similar experiments with local materials.

Students seeking a wider range should consult Bernard Leach's *A Potter's Book,* particularly for celadon glazes, Daniel Rhodes' *Clay and Glazes for the Potter* and *Stoneware and Porcelain*, and, for aspiring chemists, *Ceramic Glazes* by Felix Singer and W. L. German.

A special category of once-fired stoneware is salt glazed pottery, which is found at both extremes of the world of ceramics. It is much used by sculptural potters who admire its surface quality and range, and also by the manufacturers of drain pipes, who find it a cheap and easy way of waterproofing land drains. By shovelling common salt (sodium chloride) into the firemouth of the kiln, a skin of glaze forms from the sodium on the ware and the kiln walls alike, whilst the chlorine burns off as a poisonous gas. Needless to say, such glazes require the exclusive use of an outdoor kiln, and can only be produced in fuel-burning kilns with a flue. The resulting glaze, which forms at stoneware temperature, is mottled, varying between grey and brown with a lustrous sheen, and used to be seen on old stone ginger beer jars, as well as the famous Bellarmine ware.

Glazes with familiar qualities on one clay may reveal different characteristics on another. The combination of a translucent amber earthenware glaze on a red clay makes a pleasing rich brown, and the effect of clay slips under glazes is mentioned in Chapter 16. One glazing method which changes the qualities of the glaze considerably is raw glazing or once firing, where the glaze is put direct on to the dry green pot, and only once fired to the maturing temperature. As might be expected, the glaze becomes very closely combined with the body, and often matt in surface. Economy of firing is counterbalanced by a high risk of failure, especially when the glaze is being applied, but once-fired ware has a quality of unity and a fine tradition (see pictures on pages 1 and 50).

15 Glaze faults and remedies

Unlike the medical student who learns about the body before getting on to the general practice of curing maladies and weaknesses, most potters learn about their materials by trying to cure faults.

The short unmusical pinging of a glaze cracking on a pot fresh from the kiln is a maddening sound to the potter; it means that fine hairline cracks are appearing on a glaze, and will spread until the pot is covered with a fine network which will catch the dirt and become ever more noticeable. Encouraged in some Eastern ceramics by rubbing oxide into the cracks and refiring it is rarely thought beautiful today. A sudden change of temperature—like the shock of cold air to a pot taken too soon from the kiln—will encourage *crazing*, and it is this change of temperature which un-hygienically disfigures serving dishes, put into the oven to keep the meat warm.

The reason for this most common of glaze failures is a disharmony between the glaze and the body. Earthenware glazes are usually in a state of compression after firing, induced by the greater shrinkage of the body as it cools. If the compression is not enough, cracks will appear and spread. An absorbent unglazed base which can soak up water in the washing-up bowl will cause the body to expand very slightly, and aggravate the situation by putting the glaze under tension.

An alteration to the clay or the glaze will be necessary to prevent crazing and, oddly enough, the addition of silica in the form of flint or quartz will increase the amount of shrinkage in the body if added to the clay, and decrease the amount of glaze shrinkage if added to the glaze, effectively putting the glaze into the required state of compression in either case.

For the amateur potter it is usually more practical to adapt the glaze to suit an existing clay, and unfortunately the addition of silica will change the glaze quality, so small measured additions of silica should be added, starting with 1 per cent, and tested until the crazing fault has been cured.

In earthenware glazes borax is useful in correcting a glaze with a tendency to craze, and can even be added to glazes in which lead is the principal flux. A really good safeguard against crazing on

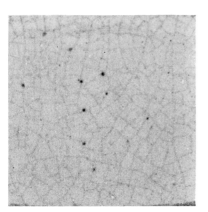

Crazing

earthenware, however, is to make sure that the body is biscuit-fired to over 1,100°C, as this causes the body to contract more at low temperatures, when the pot is subsequently glazed, giving the glaze a useful squeeze.

At stoneware temperatures the relationship between glaze and body is a very close one, since both have vitrified, and the more alike they are chemically, the less likely is crazing. Sometimes a glaze will craze even when it is well matched to the body, if it has been applied to the pot unevenly or unreasonably thickly. If the door of a glaze kiln is opened too soon the shock of cold air strikes the glaze before it reaches the clay, and will cause crazing which could otherwise be avoided. Unfortunately the temptation to open the kiln while it is still warm is a very strong one, and hard to resist.

When crazing is thought to be attractive it is graced with another name by those who admire the effect, and called 'crackle'.

Shivering, or *shelling*, is a form of crazing in which the glaze, under excessive compression, is forced away from the body and chips off, especially on edges. Too much silica in the body or the glaze is the usual cause, and it is difficult to remove the silica when the material has been prepared. The best remedy is to scrap the glaze and prepare a new one containing less flint or quartz.

Crawling is a tiresome fault with a more disastrous effect on finished ware. It is the shrinking away of the glaze from certain areas of a pot, leaving a raw scar, usually stained in colour. There are two principal causes, both curable. The presence of grease or dust on the biscuit pot leads to crawling, and the normal greasiness of fingers is enough to cause crawling on a much-handled pot. A biscuit pot with less tactile appeal may lie around on a workshop shelf for a long time attracting dust, and this has exactly the same result. If the potter suspects that the unglazed ware is either greasy or dusty it is worth biscuit firing the pot a second time, to cleanse the surface, even though it means waiting longer to see the pot finished.

Crawling is also caused if the glaze, when applied to the pot, dries out too rapidly and cracks on the surface like the mud in a dried-up puddle. Such cracking can be carefully smoothed over with the fingertips, effectively forcing powdered glaze into the fissures, and the fault may be avoided, but if a glazed pot is put into a kiln with the cracks still showing, crawling is likely, and it is very ugly. The glazing of still-warm biscuit ware will often cause cracking of the glazed surface before firing, as will the application of a second coat of the glaze. Matt glazes are more likely to crawl than shiny ones.

Blistering is an unattractive feature associated with the use of too much chromium in combination with other colouring oxides, and occurs in earthenware lead glazes if the kiln atmosphere is oxygen-starved or 'reduced' (see Chapter 18). Where the culprit is already in the glaze, the only cure is to start afresh with a new glaze, but sometimes blistering is the result of overfiring, in which case the cure is obvious.

Crawling can be caused by grease or dust on the biscuited surface.

Pinholing in a glaze is the result of volcanic activity during firing, either from the glaze 'mantle' or from the body below. Small eruptions of gases from within the glaze will leave ugly 'craters', and the cure for this is often 'soaking' the glaze, or maintaining a high kiln temperature with the glaze molten, so that an even layer of glaze will re-form over the scars. This is not a satisfactory cure, however, when the fault is in a matt glaze, as such a glaze is never very liquid on the surface of the pot.

When the eruptions come from the body they may be unsightly bloats or blisters, or they may be pock-marks on the surface, which can be quite attractive on stoneware of a certain rugged type.

Underfiring and *overfiring* are faults of kiln technique rather than of glazing. It is a sad waste of effort not to fire a carefully prepared glaze to its optimum temperature, and a difference of 10°C can make all the difference between a commonplace pot and a pot of distinction. The characteristics of underfired ware are unmistakeable: a dull dryness of surface reminiscent of an unripe pear. If it is not possible to vary the kiln temperature in an evening class firing, where the work of many students shares the same kiln, then a glaze which does not mature should be abandoned.

Overfired ware not only looks too runny and treacly, but the glaze will also probably have run into a pool inside the pot or run down the outside and stuck the pot to the kiln shelf. Gravity affects the quality of a glaze, and sometimes a glaze which holds together beautifully on a flat tile will run miserably thin if put on a pot with vertical sides. One should thus consider the shape of the pot when choosing the glaze.

Experimentation with glazes and bodies is an occupation for someone with a great deal of time to spare, and for the potter with limited time, who has laboured long over a single pot and then been disappointed by its glaze, there is a ray of hope: a second coating of glaze can be applied and the pot refired. The result of a combination of two different glazes fired at different times will look like neither, nor will it even resemble an intelligent guess at a mixture of the two. But it may be better than the original surface. To get the chosen glaze to stick to the pot, warm up the pot slightly and add a sticky substance of some kind to the glaze. Gum arabic or even sugar will help, and will not affect the glaze itself. Getting the new glaze to lie evenly over the glazed surface is not easy by the pouring method, and spraying the second coat on with an atomizer is recommended.

16
Decoration:

The raw pot

The Greeks were great 'decorators' of pottery, in the sense that they used ceramics as a vehicle for a painted design. This was at once two-dimensional, because of the flat application of colour (though often figures were shown in perspective), and three-dimensional in the way in which it filled or covered a curved surface. Sometimes the Attic pot was a masterpiece of decoration, but sometimes it was not. Never did the red, black and white design have a real unity with the materials of the pot, the fire-bound unity familiar in Oriental and Persian ceramics. The pot on page 103, an Islamic earthenware bowl some seven hundred years old, with its freely painted 'arabesque' in soft black, is the apotheosis of decoration on pottery. So superbly does the design fill and complete the surface of the bowl that it seems belittled by the very word 'decoration', which implies a treatment of a surface or an object subsequent to its making and not a part of the original concept. The West African vessel above is designed and decorated so harmoniously that one cannot state where one element ends and the other begins. The unglazed food vessels made by Indians of the Mato Grosso on page 137 show a bold improvisation of painted decoration, and above all these pots hint at the irresistability of a ceramic surface—a surface which cries out to the potter to be decorated, and decorated all over.

In previous chapters I have discussed the clothing of a pot in glaze and I hope I have emphasised that a carefully-balanced glaze alone is a fitting decoration for a finished pot. Many times I have watched a pupil, absolutely determined that his work was incomplete without a painted spray of flowers, resolutely spoil a competent pot by adding a stiff and unrelaxed piece of brushwork with no intrinsic merit and no relation to the form of the pot.

There can be no absolute rules for decoration, just as there is no longer any grammar of design. A rigid geometric pattern can succeed just as well as a free or organic ornament; a brutal or violent contortion of a pot can be as successful in its own terms as a delicately executed lacework in clay. In the following description of decorative techniques there should be no conclusions drawn as to one method's superiority over others. There is only one outstanding tenet which I would apply to the decoration of ceramics—that it should be *confidently done*, with assurance and no hesitation. The fiery atmosphere of the kiln has an unkind way of mocking tentative efforts and of making the muffed brushstroke look ridiculous, whilst it respects and underlines in the final product the emphatic mark, the clearly drawn line or the crisp-cut edge.

Impressed design

Vessel made in the form of a calabash, with incised decoration, from Cameroun.

The decoration of a pot can begin at the early stages of making, not only after the biscuit firing. While the clay is plastic, or when it is leather-hard, its surface can be decorated by impressing or embossing. The picture on page 130 shows the result of impressing everyday household objects into rolled-out clay, giving either a random pattern or a regular one (a metal nut, bicycle chain, a pipe, a block of wood). Both types can be effective if sensitively used for the plane-surfaces of slab pots. One could prepare a long list of household odds and ends which would serve this semi-automatic function, and it is important to avoid combining more than one or two impressions on a single pot. The simpler the design of the 'seal' the better, and of course effective seals can be specially made out of Plaster of Paris or wood (see overleaf). Some natural forms make good seals, and the best one I have ever come across is the seed case of the Eucalyptus tree, with a rigid star-shaped pattern on its end which is both geometric and alive. Within the pottery workshop, the beginner short of inspiration can use the ends of turning tools or Seger cones to gain practice in making repeating shapes.

A small stamp or seal like a button can look ridiculous in isolation on a pot, but used in a regular or linear way it can make a

useful focus for the eye. Such a belt or band around a thrown cylinder, for example, can most easily be made by the use of an incised roller—a home-made tool like a cotton reel made out of wood or plaster, engraved with a design, which is rolled around the thrown form leaving a pattern in its wake. Such devices are often used on thrown pots to conceal inexpert throwing, but usually they fail to do this, and simply make the pot look clumsier.

Impressed designs can be made on hand-made tiles when the tiles are at the leather-hard stage, but pressure on the tile will distort its shape and the result is only effective when the tiles do not need to be precise in size or smooth in use. The good qualities of an impressed design are often increased by the glazing. A light dusting of a colouring oxide will catch in the edges of the design and emphasise the pattern, while stoneware glazes, which usually break into a different colour on edges, will soften the contour of the impression without obliterating the design.

Embossed designs

These depend on the addition of clay to the pot's surface, and if the pot is leather-hard there will be a need for slip or water as a 'glue'. Small wads of clay impressed with seals can be added to finished pots as medallions, much like the glass labels added to the necks of old wine and port bottles.

The famous Wedgwood Jaspar ware is the classic form of embossed design, in which delicately formed porcelain or white clay designs, cast from small plaster moulds, are added to a coloured pot as bas relief—a decorative technique known as 'sprigging'. Beginners who wish to emboss designs need not strive after natural forms, which are unlikely to relate to the form of the pot to which they are

Suggested tools for impressing clay. Centre: a Eucalyptus seed case.

attached, but should consider the effect of such excrescences on the profile of the pot, and remember that simple motifs like strapwork whorls are the most striking.

Pierced designs

The leather-hard pot can also be decorated by 'piercing'. Cutting away parts of the wall is a delicate operation, and the pot must be tackled when dry enough to stand up against the cutting tool but not so dry that it will crack. Simple holes can be bored easily enough with a drill-bit held in the fingers, but other patterns have to be cut carefully with a sharp pointed blade like a dissector's scalpel, and the more holes the weaker the structure. Very small holes will fill in with glaze when fired, a common Oriental technique much borrowed by European potters. More effective is a design in which the cut-away areas remain open, as in the pot by Ian Godfrey below.

A Plaster of Paris seal with an incised design will make a raised pattern when pressed against clay. A panel of clay decorated in this way has been applied to one of the sides of the slab pot above by Ian Auld.

Right: perforated bowl by Ian Godfrey. Below: a pattern being incised in the surface of a coil pot from Tanzania.

Incised, fluted and faceted designs

These are all decorative techniques which reach perfection in Oriental pottery. Incised patterns can be very simple or tremendously intricate, and the cutting back of layers of clay within a concave surface such as a bowl demands high standards of crafts-manship. Most low-relief incised work is combined with slip, described later in the chapter.

Fluting, often spiral but effective when vertical, is well suited to the beginner. A cylindrical form may be fluted from top to base, like a Doric column, using a loop-ended wire tool as shown in the diagram. Such a tool is very effective if made from banding wire, which can be formed into the desired shape and will stay in shape when in use. If the fluting is only going to cover part of the pot the termination of the flutes must be clearly defined by a shoulder or the reduced diameter of the foot sharpened up, if necessary, by turning.

Faceting is a basic design exercise as well as a decoration for a simple pot. A thick-walled cylinder can be made into an interesting shape if the outside surface is cut into facets with a sharp knife. Mathematical figures and crystal structures are obvious sources of inspiration for potters who are primarily interested in the form of their pots, but these are most conveniently made out of slabs.

Any decorative technique which involves the slicing or gouging of clay will be modified if the clay body is coarse or contains a great deal of grog. Striations and granular surfaces are attractive in robust and stout stoneware, but unsuitable for earthenware where a smooth clay should be used for any incised work.

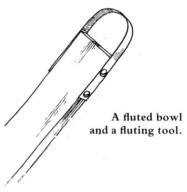

**A fluted bowl
and a fluting tool.**

An incised design forms an important part of this porcelain wall panel by Eileen Nisbet.

Inlaying

Decoration which is carried out on leather-hard or plastic pots is not restricted to changes in surface. Colour can be added at this stage either by inlaying or in the form of slip. Lino-cutting tools or similar gouging knives can be used to cut a pattern in leather-hard clay much as a pattern is cut in lino.

A coloured body clay can be impressed into an incised design, provided the coloured clay is soft enough to fill up the incised areas without distorting the edges. As it dries, the surface of the pot can be scraped down to reveal the inlay as a crisp design. This technique is not confined to detailed and fine line patterns, and when used boldly is a particularly powerful method of decorating, since it becomes part of the fabric of the pot under the glaze and not merely a superficial layer.

Slip decoration

Slipware is, in its simplest form, pottery in which the body is treated with a thin layer of clay of a different colour. The decorative layer is applied in a very liquid form, like a glaze, by pouring over the clay body which should be in a soft leather-hard state, and the finished pot is coated with a transparent glaze. Most frequently, a coloured slip is used to cover the inside of bowls, and this is the starting point of a whole range of decorative techniques.

Decoration slip is prepared by softening clay to a creamy consistency with water, and sieving through an 80 or 100 mesh lawn, together with colourants if the slip is to be darkened. A good black can be made with 15 per cent of iron oxide plus 3 per cent of cobalt or manganese, while 2 per cent each of copper and cobalt will make a strong peacock blue. If the body clay is red, a dense black slip can be made by adding 5 per cent cobalt oxide to the dry weight of the red clay. The clay for the slip should be that of the body of the pot, though this is not possible when the pot is made of red clay, and the slip is to be white. In this case a good white slip can be made out of china clay (3 parts), ball clay (1 part) and feldspar (1 part), or ball clay (4 parts) and china clay (1 part). A white slip, which must of necessity differ from the coloured body on to which it will be poured, may not be a very good 'fit' and you may have to try several recipes before finding one which matches the expansion and contraction curve of your particular body clay. Cracks on the surface of the slip as it dries on to the pot are a warning sign, but the scaling off, like the crazing of a glaze, may not appear until the pot has been fired.

Like glazes and the casting slips mentioned in Chapter 11, decorative slips must be kept smooth and even in texture, and the addition of bentonite as a suspender may help. The deflocculants used in casting slips are not necessary as the shrinkage of slip and body should be the same. The best method of keeping a slip in good

Brush-painted slip decoration.

condition, however, is to sieve it regularly—always before use—and to keep it in a bucket *with a lid*.

All shapes of pot can be 'slipped', in the same way as they can be glazed, by dipping and pouring, but the leather-hard pot will readily disintegrate in the bucket if kept immersed for too long, and the slipping of a very thin shallow bowl is difficult, for the walls are always fragile until the pot has been fired.

The most fruitful use of slip for the beginner is in combination with a press-mould for here the walls of the pot are supported by the mould until the whole thing is dry. The pictures show two slips being used in quick succession, one all over the bowl, the other over part of the surface only, and the mould then being rolled around so that a marbled pattern is produced.

A less random design is produced by running lines of contrasting slip into a slip layer or 'field' and drawing them into a delicate feathered pattern by running a fine point, the tip of a feather, or single bristle across the lines at right angles (see opposite). A many-toothed tool can be used to 'comb' contrasting slips into striking patterns.

White slip, then black slip, poured on to a bowl in a press mould, make a marbled design when the bowl is tilted and rolled around.

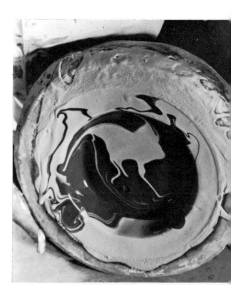

The distinctive patterns made by drawing a feather or a sharp point through alternating lines of coloured slip.

Dots of coloured slip applied to the Plaster of Paris wall will form an inlayed pattern in a bowl cast from this mould.

Once immersed in the world of slip, the beginner can experiment with many techniques, more or less creative, which depend on the reluctance of two different coloured liquids to lose their separate identity, like cream in black coffee. To say that there is a danger of slip decoration becoming automatic and lifeless is to invite the scorn and wrath of those who admire the famous slipware dishes of the seventeenth and eighteenth centuries. By squeezing slip of the right consistency from a plastic or rubber bag by means of a fine nozzle, the inventive potter has at his command a means of drawing in liquid clay. Somewhere midway between the weaponry of the political cartoonist and the folk-artistry of the iced-cake decorator lies the particular charm of slip-trailing. The bag and nozzle, which is the only tool needed, can be bought from any pottery supplier, or improvised.

Drawing with slip demands a strong colour contrast (white on black, brown on white) and a stiffer mix than for the feathered and combed techniques, with the lines standing out in relief even when dry and fired. If a slip surface or ground is used over the inside of a bowl this should be allowed to dry to a non-tacky state before the slip-trailing is added.

Slip painting and sgraffito

So far the decorative slip methods described, like glazing techniques, do not show the mark of a tool, but slip can be applied to a leather-hard pot like paint with a brush, or scratched away, like scraper-

Left and below: decoration in black slip painted with a brush over white slip. Pottery by Karen Foster.

board, with a sharp tool, showing the contrasting clay below. Painted slip, usually applied with a large mop-headed brush, will show marks of the paintbrush when it has been fired, and these are often attractive if bold and big, and the reverse if they are small and repetitive. Big splashy patterns can be bounded by regular banding lines to give the decoration a more controlled appearance, as the bowl in the illustrations shows. Because of the unevenness of the coating, painted slip is not suitable as a ground to feathering or trailing, and is best left alone or used in combination with *sgraffito*. Any sharp tool such as a penknife or turning tool will scratch through the surface of a leather-hard slip revealing the contrasting colour of the leather-hard clay below. It is a hard, non-fluid technique, and attracts the in-artistic. Lamentable examples of sgraffito work abound, with monochromatic heraldic shields, cartoons and mottoes leading the field. Drawing with a point is much less flexible than drawing with

a pencil, but lettering, if it is noble Roman or Uncial lettering, can be very impressive if incised through slip, especially if the potter tackles the fascinating typographical problem of letters in a roundel.

Other methods of decorating with slip include the use of wax and stencils, and these will be described in the next chapter, with majolica decoration.

Slipware is traditionally an earthenware form, finished with a glossy transparent glaze. Through the glaze the slip, dull and matt when it is being applied, shows its true colours, often enhanced with richness and depth. Pots destined to be stoneware can be slipped when leather-hard, and they are often left without a glaze, in which case the surface is called an 'engobe'. Such pots can have an interesting texture (see pages 50 and 80), but are not very practical if the surface is rough, as they attract dust and are very difficult to clean.

Painting with oxides

The same oxides that colour glazes can be painted on to a raw un-fired pot with a brush, or sponged on to a hand-built pot which has a coarse surface texture. These powdered oxides, even if mixed with gum arabic or some other paste, are very susceptible to smudging until they have been fired, and when the pots come out of the biscuit kiln the colour will be disappointingly muted and dry. It is only in or under a glaze that oxide colours shine out brightly, and most decoration with oxides takes place after the biscuit firing.

A bat, a hawk, a turtle, a star. Variations on a simple form made by Waura Indians of the Mato Grosso, Brazil.

17
Decoration:

Biscuit and glazed pots

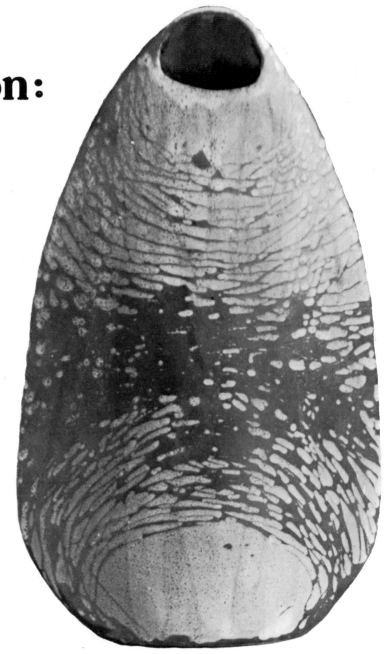

A dark glaze under a light one, revealed by sgraffito after the first glaze firing. Pot by James Tower.

In the minds of many beginners, decorating the biscuit pot conjures up images of a paintbrush loaded with colourant poised shakily over an absorbent biscuit surface which will readily and permanently soak up any drops which accidentally fall. The decoration stage means a re-acquaintance with a small paintbrush and a tussle with the formal elements of design, but painted-on decoration is only one of many ways in which a biscuit-fired pot may be ornamented, and some of the more automatic techniques should be learned first by the beginner in order to gain confidence in the handling of ware at this stage.

The glaze itself is the only decoration needed if the form of the pot is irregular or without convenient surfaces to contain a design (see page 86). One glaze laid on top of another will create a contrast, especially if the glazes used are widely different. A popular way of avoiding the issue of deliberate design is to pour a dark glaze over a part of a pot already glazed in a light colour, allowing the trickles to remain as they have run. The suet pudding and chocolate sauce effect which results unfortunately has a very disruptive effect on the form and profile of the pot, and is only tolerable if the pot is a single strong shape.

Controlled glazing is more satisfying. Imagine dipping a shallow bowl vertically up to half way—to its widest point—in a bucket of glaze. When this is dry, the other half can be dipped into a contrasting glaze so that the two lines of glaze just meet. When again dry, the bowl could be dipped into a third glaze, this time at 90° to the previous dips, so that the design on the face of the bowl is 'quartered' and the four segments of the circle will be a different colour. Even if the second glaze is used again for the third dip, there will still be four different surfaces, since one of them is a double thickness.

Contrasting glazes can be used alternately, with overlaps, to make stripes of different colour or texture on slab pots or thrown shapes as shown in the pictures, and advantage can be taken of the curved shape which results from a bowl or slab form being inserted into a bowl of glaze at an angle. This technique, known as 'window dipping' is often effective on simple shapes and the potter will soon learn that a glaze which is allowed to make its own 'edge' will often have a more natural appearance than a demarcation which is drawn or etched with a tool.

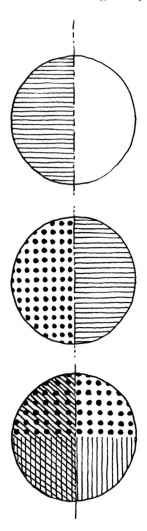

A bowl or plate 'quartered' with three glazes; the first shown by straight lines, the second by dots, the third by diagonal lines.

Many glazes change their character according to the thickness of application. Variations in colour and texture, especially on stoneware, often give the pot all the decoration that is needed, as in this bowl by Janet Leach.

Dipping a pot as shown produces a central stripe where glazes overlap.

Glazes will adhere to biscuit ware and to one another, but they will shrink away from oily surfaces and if wax or a similar substance is painted on to the pot, or between glazes, the next water-bound liquid which is poured on will shrink away from the waxed areas. When the wax, left bare, burns away in the kiln it leaves behind its own pattern. If this seems a long-winded technique for achieving a negative result, remember that painting with glaze is unsatisfactory and the only way of getting a glaze to go around, say, an oak-leaf shape is to have something in the way, preventing the glaze sticking to the surface where the design is.

Scraping away the glaze is one method, like the sgraffito method with slip, but it is not satisfactory where large areas are concerned, and impossible where one glaze overlies another if both of them are in their unfired form.

It is difficult to paint detailed designs with hot wax, as it dries on the surface of the pot very quickly. It is better to plan a simple design.

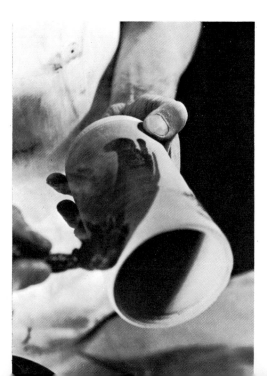

The glaze will not stick where the wax has been applied.

Wax for this work is prepared by putting a plain white candle broken up into short lengths into a small pan with turpentine or paraffin, and heating very gently until the wax is all melted. Fierce heating may cause the material to catch fire in the pan, and for safety this is best done in a double saucepan, or in a bowl in a saucepan of water. A visible and evil-smelling smoke is a healthy sign that the mixture is warm and of a watery consistency which makes it easier to use. The wax will dry and 'freeze' as soon as it is painted on to the pot or glaze surface, which restricts the type of design which can be successfully applied. If the pot to be decorated can be warmed, the working life of the wax will be a little longer.

One disadvantage of this method is the disastrous effect the hot wax has on brushes, which can never be cleaned satisfactorily and will quickly lose their hairs if left in the liquid for long. The picture sequence shows a very coarse 'brush' made from string used to make a broad mark on the side of a pot. The wax resist technique is very distinctive, as the glaze shrinks away from the grease in an attractive way, often leaving behind small globules of glaze which fire on to the pot as spots. It is also a practical method of keeping rims and feet clear when pouring glaze and a wax resist ring in the centre of a bowl will allow another pot with an unglazed foot ring to be stacked inside it in the glaze firing, a practical way of avoiding waste space and often successful aesthetically. When wax is painted straight on to the biscuit surface, rather than on top of a glaze, the resulting raw area will be porous if the pot is only fired to earthenware temperature, and vessels intended to hold liquids will be useless if decorated in this way on their inside surfaces.

Wax is not the only material which can come between glaze and ware. Cut-out paper patterns, cloth or scrim will have the same effect, and vine leaves or other leaves with an interesting form can be used direct. When such solid materials are used, however, they

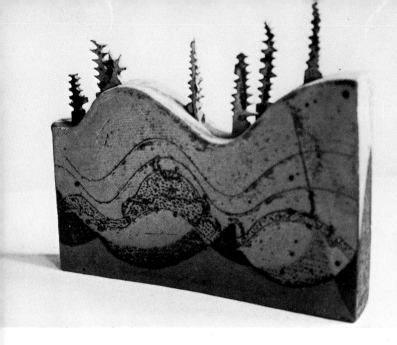

A slab landscape with matt glaze, by Bryan Newman.

Paper-resist design on a bowl by Jane Hamlyn.

should be pulled off the pot before it is fired, as the glaze which sticks to them would make a mess of the pot or the kiln shelf. All these 'resist' techniques are admirably suited to slip decoration on raw pots as well as on biscuit ware. The damp surface of the raw pot helps the adhesion of the paper pattern, while on biscuit pots it often has to be kept in place with some form of glue or paste, especially on vertical surfaces.

Other slip techniques such as trailing through a nozzle and sgraffito can be tried with glaze, though the results will be quite different, since glaze when molten is more mobile than slip, and will flow somewhat, reducing the width of an incised line.

The melting glaze has an effect on all linear and painted patterns, and *under-glaze* and *on-glaze* are terms which are often heard, reflecting techniques and taste, and sometimes confusing the beginner. The distinctions are simple, though the results are very wide ranging, and can occasionally confound the connoisseur. A

On-glaze decoration. The design is painted in blue-green, purple and brown on top of a white tin glaze. Bowl by Alan Caiger-Smith.

transparent glaze applied over a design will blur it to some extent, depending on the stability of the materials used for the design. If an opaque glaze, white or coloured, is used over a design it will obscure it much more, to the extent of hiding it altogether if the glaze is a very dense one.

A design applied on top of the glaze will not be blurred or obscured though it may 'float' slightly at the edges as the glaze melts, and the quality of the painted surface may differ from the rest, since it lies on the top.

It is quite a considerable shock to a designer already competent with a fine sable brush when he first encounters the 'feel' of painting on absorbent clay or glaze. The ware sucks the liquid out of the hairs, and forces the designer to develop a light touch or the brush will dry against the pot and leave a mean and unattractive mark. This is why potters' brushes (some of which, with their characteristic marks, are shown below) are longer and more straggly than painters' brushes.

The beginner will gain confidence with a brush if he applies bands of colour to a cylinder, by holding the brush steady against the pot and rotating the pot in the centre of a banding wheel or wheel-head. Other painted designs should be kept simple and bold, and restricted to one or two colours.

Ceramic suppliers are very ready to provide colouring stains for painting in a wide range of hues and tints, calling them under-glaze or 'decoration' colours. Most studio potters prefer to make their own colours by using the same metal oxides as are mixed into glazes, finely ground and mixed with water, or water and gum. Since these metal oxides are mostly leaden grey or black in colour, a sample pot or tile should be painted with a stripe of each oxide available in the workshop, carefully named, and ideally these should be tested both under and over each glaze which is used.

Such a programme of testing would certainly occupy an evening-class student's entire term, but once made, the results can be shared and there is no better way of getting to know the potential of colourants. Most oxides burn through stoneware glazes at high temperatures, if they are applied before the glaze, but at earthenware temperatures they are more likely to be concealed or blurred. This is not necessarily a disadvantage, but it is important that a blurred result suits the style of the design. To avoid the smudging of an under-glaze design, some potters go to the length of firing decorated biscuit pots without glaze, and re-firing a glaze coat later. This avoids the dragging of the design by the glaze on application, and it also prevents the adulteration of the glaze itself with colour from the design. Painting with unfixed under-glaze colour or oxides on biscuit pots is slightly anti-social in communal potteries, where spots of colour pulled from the pattern by the glaze as it is being poured stay in the glaze bucket to alter the mix. On the other hand, under-glaze designs, as exemplified by the pot on page 103, have a quality of permanence which is unattainable by any other means.

Above: banding, with a long brush or 'liner'. Below: brushes, with their typical marks.

In evening classes the most convenient stage at which to apply painted decoration is after the pouring of the glaze, and before the firing. Both glaze and pattern are very vulnerable to handling at this point, and whilst application is not difficult, smudging or fingermarking of the design is all too easy, and the potter should handle the ware as little as possible.

On-glaze painting is the technique used in the famous majolica ware of Italy, where a design predominantly in blue is painted over a white tin glaze on an earthenware body. Though they reached their peak in the sixteenth century, freely painted designs of this type are still made in Mediterranean countries for domestic ware such as plates and serving bowls. As far as I am concerned such joyful but humble pottery makes northern European industrial attempts to bring liveliness to the everyday dining table seem quite pathetic and graceless. In Britain, the Aldermaston pottery of Alan Caiger-Smith upholds a tradition for rhythmically painted majolica ware, using wax resist enamel and lustre techniques as part of a highly distinctive range.

The later in the sequence of making a pot that a painted design is applied, the more superficial it appears, and some surfaces applied after the glaze firing eventually wear away with use. Two important

Left: jar with painted lustre design, by Alan Caiger-Smith.

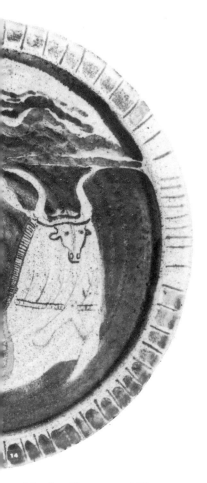

Metal oxides are used like water-colours to provide the design on this bowl by Eric Mellon. The thicker the coating of oxide, the darker the colour. Ash glaze is then poured over the pot and the design burns through in the kiln.

decorative techniques which must be applied after the glaze firing are enamelling and lustre, since both are essentially low-fired techniques, the maturing temperature being lower than the temperature of the glaze.

Enamel colours, which are also available from ceramic suppliers, are mixed with turpentine or an oil mixture as a medium, and the technique of painting on the glazed pot or tile closely resembles the ornamentation of other non-ceramic materials. Extremely fine and detailed designs can be painted on to glazed surfaces, and for some would-be potters painting pictures on ready-made ware is a satisfying occupation, though it certainly does not give them much experience of ceramics. Enamels are fired to about 750°C, and similar temperatures are used today for lustre ware.

Lustre is a form of decoration in which a film of metal is laid on top of the glaze. Most potters encounter lustre as a liquid preparation for on-glaze painting containing such metallic salts as copper sulphate which, when burnished after firing, becomes a very convincing 'gold'. Lustre can also be mixed with low-temperature glazes to give an all-over metallic sheen as well as painted on to fired glazed ware, but it should not be mixed with other ware in the kiln. It is very sensitive to the atmosphere in the kiln, which can make the result unburnishable. Some lustre preparations require a reducing atmosphere, and this was true of Persian and Moorish lustres of the early Middle Ages.

The techniques of decoration so far described do not help the potter who wants to be able to repeat a design exactly on many pieces of ware. In industry, printing is used with ceramic colourants instead of inks, and designs can either be 'transferred' to the ware on a thin transparent film which burns away in the kiln, or printed direct on to the pot through a silk screen. Many studio potters borrow and combine these methods from industry, and using a silk-screen printing press, print in one or more colours on to a film with a paper backing. The backing can be floated off in water, and the design fixed on to the glazed surface of a plate, a cup or a tile. Flat surfaces are best, of course, for keeping the design intact.

Direct screen printing (i.e. with the ware directly under the screen) must be done on to a perfectly flat surface, and ready-made tiles have a rounded 'cushion' edge which will spoil the quality of a direct screen print which has to cover the whole surface.

It is a worth-while experiment in evening schools which have facilities for both screen printing and pottery to get together, as often happens in art schools, so that the work of silk-screen designers can be permanently fired on to pottery. Screen printing allows solid areas of flat colour with a very precise edge, and it is possible to reproduce photographs and detailed designs with great accuracy. The enamel colours used in ceramic screen printing are very bright, and are most successfully printed on top of a white glazed surface for contrast. The technique is equally appropriate for small discrete patterns, and large repeating designs.

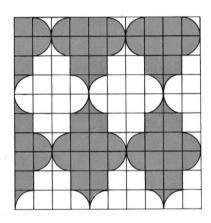

Radial design by Alan Wallwork, made by dropping spots of glaze on to a tile.

Tile picture by Maggie Berkowitz.

Only two designs, in different colours, are required to make the tile pattern below.

Geometric and diaper patterns on tiles are often made by the assembly of four or more different units in such a way as to give a large-scale repeating pattern—the diagram shows such a design on a tile frame five feet square made from just two tile variations, and two colours. Repetition, however, is not an essential part of design and decoration with tiles. The tile is a convenient manufacturing unit by which an original painting the size of the entire west-front of a cathedral can be made permanent by the high-temperature ceramic process. One of the most inspiring examples I know of the use of tiles for giant wall paintings is the Dominican Chapel at Vence, near Nice, designed and executed by Matisse.

The decoration and design of tiles is a vast subject on its own, daunting to the amateur yet fascinating to many beginners. Tile-making has been mentioned in Chapter 10, and is both a lengthy and frustrating business when the potter lacks tile-making equipment. Thick stoneware and relief tiles can be successfully made, however, and it is worth remembering that they need not be square—only interlocking to make an effective cladding. Hand-made tiles can have a textured surface or, like any other ceramics, can be impressed, incised or inlaid before they are dried and fired. If they are to make a practical flat surface like the top of a coffee table, however, the surface must be smooth and the best way of decorating the surface is to use metal oxides or on-glaze enamels on plain white glazed tiles. It is difficult to find glazes to fit the body material of unglazed tiles without crazing and it is also quite difficult to find a manufacturer of tiles who will supply them without glaze.

Bands, drops and spots of earthenware glaze can be arranged on glazed tile surfaces to great effect, as shown in the photograph above, which is a complete design within itself as well as a strong single element for use in a decorative panel. Beginners should remember that a single well-decorated tile can look lost or downright ugly when combined with other tiles in a wall surface, and if the amateur has the perseverance to make a tile panel he must plan the total design in advance, and resist being distracted by detail.

18 Kilns and kiln firing

The average pot has a double encounter with the kiln, once for biscuit and once for glaze firing, as explained in Chapter 1. The average beginner will probably not encounter the kiln at all, for his pots are fired for him, and the techniques of kiln loading and operating remain a mystery.

All too often inadequate, small kilns or broken electric kiln elements cause a bottleneck in the flow of students' work, and a pot, after waiting a fortnight or so to be biscuit fired, will wait again for a glaze kiln, and its vulnerable decorated surface may become damaged, chipped or finger-marked. Moments of delight, when a perfect finished pot appears from the kiln, occur to compensate for the disappointments of waiting and damage, but the beginner learns that a pot's path through the kiln may be far from swift and straightforward, and understanding the sequence of events can sometimes help to counteract impatience.

In the 1980's a revolution based on space technology has completely changed the hardware involved in the firing of pottery both in industry and for the studio potter. It is the introduction of ceramic fibre which provides a high degree of insulation and dramatically reduces the cost of firing whatever source of energy is used. A brief resumé of the effect of this new material follows later in this chapter, but the principles of firing remain and are worth describing first. A kiln is basically a rigid chamber, either temporary or permanent, which must be able to withstand high temperatures without changing shape, and designed so that energy can be applied either by electricity, gas, oil or wood to concentrate the heat evenly in the chamber. This is achieved by the layout of elements (in an electric kiln) or by the routeing of draughts or fire pathways when combustible fuel is used. In the latter case, care is sometimes taken to prevent the pottery or ware coming into direct contact with the flame by stacking it inside protective refractory cylinders called 'saggars' or by packing the pots into a sealed area or 'muffle' in the chamber around which the flames play, but into which they cannot enter. The area immediately around fuel burners and elements is hotter than anywhere else, and it is not a good place to stand a pot.

Heat rises, of course, and equally obviously a fire burns hotter when there is a good draught. Chimney design and design of the firemouth are just two aspects of the search for greater efficiency in the truly fascinating history of kiln design. The pattern of heat flow through the kiln influences the form of the outside, and the traditional bottle-oven of The Potteries is a good example of this. These ovens, like factory chimneys, are usually demolished when they are no longer used and are, alas, extremely rare. Any such large-scale oven which has to be laboriously packed, heated and cooled cannot match for efficiency a tunnel kiln, in which the thermal conditions remain constant—hot in the middle and cool at both ends—and the pottery is drawn slowly through on refractory wagons, or a clamp kiln which is lowered over ware which has been pre-stacked on a refractory base.

This kind of system is justified where there is large and continuous production. A studio potter or evening class is equipped with a chamber kiln, using energy only when it is needed .Recent developments have led to an increase in the use of kilns loaded from the top, sealed with a lid, though many kiln chambers are packed from the side and closed with a door. The method of packing is the same whatever type of kiln is used.

It is wasteful to leave any empty space inside the kiln chamber, and so small pots are arranged in layers on stout but mobile shelves. These shelves, and the tubular props which support them, are called the 'kiln furniture' and they must be capable of withstanding high temperatures without changing shape. If the structural props and shelves collapse during a firing most of the ware is destroyed, especially in the case of glost firing, as pots will probably be glued together by the glaze. The kiln shelves, made of sillimanite, are therefore strong and heavy, and the props interlock with one another for stability.

By means of the furniture a staging of pots can be built right up to the very top of the kiln. Pottery undergoing biscuit firing can be tightly packed, with pots touching, and small pots stacked inside large ones. Bowls are wasteful of space when placed side by side on a shelf, and can be stacked vertically rim to rim, a method which helps them to keep a level top. Strong pots can stand one on another but shallow or thin ware such as wide flat dishes should not have to bear weight, especially on unsupported rims. It is tempting to fill corners of a biscuit kiln by stacking plates on their edges, but unfortunately this can cause a warping or cracking of the plate. Unfired ware can be placed up against the sides of a muffle in a gas or oil kiln but they should not approach closer than $\frac{1}{2}$ inch (1 cm) to electric elements. If the elements are touched by the ware, they may burn out and melt, damaging the kiln wall at the same time. Not only the walls but the shelves themselves must be kept in good condition. Protection of shelves with batwash or 'placing powder' is described later in relation to glaze firings, but it is important in

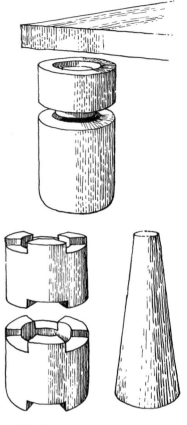

Kiln furniture

biscuit firings to avoid using shelves which are spotted with glaze.

When fired, the pots will have shrunk again—there being a total shrinkage of 10–12 per cent from the wet plastic state, depending on the type of clay. Because of the variations in the amount of shrinkage it is quite possible for one pot to become trapped inside another (which has shrunk more) during the firing, and such possibilities have to be considered when the kiln is packed.

The main cause of damage in the firing of green ware, however, is dampness. If any moisture remains in the clay it will turn into steam when the kiln temperature is raised above boiling point, and expand, cracking the pot apart. It is dampness in the centre of the thick walls of a heavy pot which causes explosions, not the thickness itself. Colour (light when dry) and feel (cool to the touch when still damp) are clues to the dryness of a pot, but if all the ware packed into a biscuit kiln seems absolutely bone dry, it is still important to start the heating process very slowly and to leave open the bung-holes and spy hole to let any steam escape. Most potters check to find out when a biscuit kiln has stopped 'steaming' by periodically holding a piece of glass over the spy hole for a few seconds to see if there is any condensation.

As the temperature inside rises, the colour will change first to a dull red, then to cherry-red, to orange and on towards white. Colours are precise indicators of temperature, but unfortunately a potter's eyes are too used to adjusting to varying light brightness to be able to relate the colour and temperature by observation. He uses two principal aids. A pyrometer is a gauge measuring temperature on a calibrated dial by means of an electric current discharged between two metals, protected inside the kiln by an insulated sleeve. The advantage of a pyrometer is that the temperature can be read off from a distance without looking inside the kiln, but it is notoriously inaccurate within about 30°C, and this is too big a margin of error for the potter. It also indicates only the temperature, rather than the work done by the heat.

A long burst of sustained heat achieves more work on a pot or a glaze than the mere temperature might suggest, and the tool used to measure this by all studio potters is the 'Seger cone'. These cones are slender pyramids about 3 inches (7 cm) long, made of ceramic mixtures designed to melt at certain precise temperatures. Shaped to stand at a slight angle to the vertical, Seger cones are often used in threes, standing in a specially shaped trough on a kiln shelf, close to the spy hole. The drawing shows a typical arrangement after firing. Cone No. 1 bends over in a gentle curve at 1,100°C, whilst

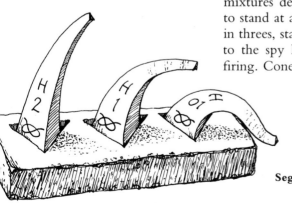

Seger cones after a firing

its neighbour No. 2 (bending at 1,120°C) remains almost upright, and its other neighbour No. 01 (1,080°C) has melted completely. Such a trio proves that the kiln has been fired to 1,100°C, no more and no less.

The cones should not be placed too close to the spy hole, and they are not always easy to position. A kiln with a hinged door will exclude all light when the door is closed, and when the kiln is being packed cold it is often useful to shut an electric torch inside the kiln to check that the cones are at the right level and visible through the spy hole. Cones are difficult to see at high temperatures when the light from inside the kiln is too bright, and staring too long through the spy hole, or too close, can become painful. Sun-glasses help, but plastic ones are inclined to melt in front of one's eyes, which gives some idea of the heat coming out as one looks in to see the state of the firing.

Biscuit firings for stoneware are usually taken to a temperature of 1,000°C, which provides a good porous surface for the application of the glaze. Industrial earthenware, however, which is often glazed to a temperature around 1,060°C, will always be biscuit fired to above 1,100°C, as a chemical change at this temperature is the cause of a state of compression in the final glaze which makes the pots more hardwearing and more resistant to crazing (see Chapter 15).

Evening class work is usually biscuit fired all together, whether it is destined to be stoneware or earthenware, and the temperature of this first firing may vary between 960° and 1,120°C. The correct sequence of firing the biscuit kiln is as follows. The kiln should be started on low for two or three hours, with the bung and spy hole open for any water vapour to escape. The kiln should be stepped up to about half power for another two or three hours, during which time the escape of vapour will cease and the bungs can be closed. The final stage of the firing—perhaps another three hours or so, depending on the kiln capacity—can be completed under full power. Thus the temperature curve for biscuit is at first gentle, then steep. The curve for the second or glost firing is the opposite—steep at first, then slow as the temperature approaches the melting point of the glaze.

Both the packing and the precise temperature are much more crucial for the glaze firing than for the biscuit firing. Since glaze, at the peak of the firing, is a liquid, it can run down and even off a pot altogether. Certainly pots glazed on the base would glue themselves glassily to the kiln shelf if allowed to stand on it. Glazed pots will also stick to one another and the kiln packer must keep them apart, at least ¼ inch (5 mm) for safety, and he must make sure that all glazed bases are lifted from the shelves on 'stilts'—the small refractory tripods with fine points which hold up the pot like finger-tips (see drawing). Stilts are not strong enough to withstand stoneware temperatures without buckling or causing the pot to buckle, and so stoneware pots stand directly on the shelf, but with no glaze

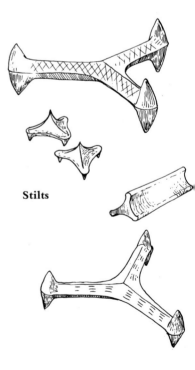

Stilts

A gas kiln dur-
ing a firing.

on or near their feet. A light sprinkling of the shelf with quartz or a proprietary 'placing powder' will prevent any sticking, but care must be taken to avoid dusting this on to the pots already stacked on lower shelves. Old kiln shelves can be painted over with a mixture of flint and water as a 'batwash' to serve the same purpose.

Variations in the behaviour of glaze in the kiln are dealt with in Chapter 15 but it is worth mentioning here that no two kiln firings are alike, and any pots which are intended to match one another in colour, texture and feel should be put in the same firing, and preferably grouped in the same area of the kiln. This is particularly important in fuel-burning kilns, where the kiln 'atmosphere' can be varied by the operator.

Reduced and oxidised firings

In earthenware, as in biscuit kilns, there is no decorative benefit to be gained by changing the kiln atmosphere, but a reducing, or oxygen-starved, atmosphere in a stoneware glaze kiln darkens the colour of the body clay which in turn changes the colour of the glaze. It also has a dramatic effect on some of the metal oxides, drawing oxygen out of them to help in the combustion process. Thus copper is changed from green to coppery red, and iron from brown to green.

By reducing the supply of oxygen in the fuel burners of kilns without or with only partial muffles, or introducing through the spy hole of a muffle kiln something (like mothballs or firewood) which will combine with or absorb oxygen in burning is a simple way of getting a reduction, though most home kiln-firers are un-certain how much wood they need, and at what temperature and for how long to sustain the reducing atmosphere. A steady supply of wood chips of the size used for firelighting should be fed into the kiln throughout the reducing period, so there must be plenty of wood handy. Half an hour is a minimum period and it is pointless to do it at all at temperatures below 1,000°C, but because it is sometimes difficult to get the kiln temperature to increase much while the atmosphere inside the kiln is oxygen-starved, a short final burst of normal (i.e. oxidising) fire is needed afterwards to reach maturing temperature.

A precise technical description of reduced stoneware firings may seem unnecessarily specialised to the beginner, but it is important for him to know why similar glazes can yield different qualities, and something of the method which has produced the most har-monious and beautiful works of Oriental art. The electric-kiln potter has the reducing technique denied to him, for successful reductions are hard to achieve in electric kilns where there is no combustion or air current, and burning materials have a harmful effect on electric elements, shortening their life.

Though some potters are content to leave the entire firing cycle in the hands of their teacher or a technician, to others the pyro-

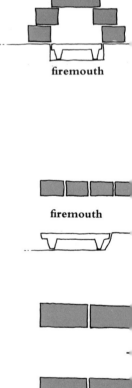

firemouth

firemouth

A simple solid fuel kiln for home building: sections and plan.

technics of pottery-making are its most fascinating part, and their enthusiasm is stirred rather than daunted by the prospect of building and firing their own kiln. There is an undeniable sense of pioneering in doing this, though in reality one is returning to a long-established tradition still practised in small potteries in many countries. Bernard Leach, in *A Potter's Book*, wrote:

> The firing is the climax of the potter's labour, and in a wood-fired kiln of any size it is a long and exhausting process. Weeks and months of hard work are at stake. Any one of a dozen things may go wrong. Wood may be damp, flues may get choked, bungs of saggars fall, shelves give way and alter the draughts, packing may have been too greedily close, or for sheer exhaustion one may have snatched an hour's sleep, handing over control to someone else and thereby altering the rhythm of the stoking. At white heat things begin to move, to warp and to bend, the roar of combustion takes on a deeper note—the heavy domes crack and tongues of white flame dart out here and there, the four-minute stokes fill the kiln shed with bursts of dense black smoke and fire. Even in the East, where hand work is usual and labour specialised, a big kiln firing has the aspect of a battlefield where men test themselves to the utmost against odds. This may sound like discouragement, but it is no more than the simple truth.

The amateur potter need not build a large kiln like this which is exhausting to fire, and most permanent home-built kilns are gas, electric or oil fired, unlike the wood-burning kiln described by Bernard Leach. There are, however, several kinds of simple solid-fuel-burning kilns which can easily be made provided one has an outdoor space in which to site them. The first is simply a brazier—a metal canister or large tin punched with air holes all round and at all levels. Filled with fairly densely packed sawdust in which are buried the pottery forms like presents in a bran tub, such a 'kiln' will reach a temperature of 750°C by being lit from the top and allowed to burn slowly downwards. Dried peat used instead of sawdust reaches about the same temperature.

A rather more complicated but temporary kiln can be made with fire bricks and a 'muffle' consisting of a single saggar or a cylinder with a base and a lid made from a 1 inch thick slab of fireclay, shaped around a chimney pot or broad drain pipe. Naturally there is a problem here if no kiln is available in which to fire the muffle before its use in the temporary kiln, and so a ready-made saggar, bought with the firebricks from a supplier, is best.

A tunnel firemouth is made of firebricks, leading to a circular chamber of firebricks in which the muffle is placed raised on bricks above the level of the 'fireplace' in the tunnel. An even circulation of air around the muffle must be ensured, and the circular chamber should be reduced in diameter towards the top to increase the draught and the temperature, the walls being sealed with clay to

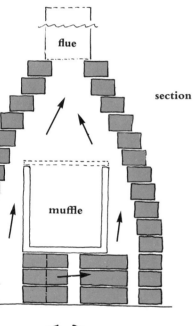

section

flue

muffle

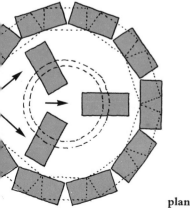

plan

prevent cold air being drawn in. This kiln, shown in the diagram, is a miniature bottle oven and fired with wood or coke will reach an adequate temperature for low biscuit, soft glaze or enamel. By smearing clay over the junctions of the bricks a better seal and up-draught is achieved.

The prospect of buying the right quantities of firebricks, tapered arch bricks, insulating bricks, common bricks and heavy ironwork to hold the finished frame corseted together has deterred many potters fortunate enough to have space available from building their own kiln, though plans are available in such books as Daniel Rhodes' *Kilns: Design, Construction and Operation* and Ian Gregory's *Kiln Building*.

If you are going to make salt glazed pottery (see Chapter 14) you have to assign a special kiln to it outdoors because of the poisonous fumes given off by the salt. Sodium chloride in the kiln coats not only the pots but the kiln walls with the glaze, and this wall coating will revolatilize when the kiln is next fired, and cover whatever is in the kiln so that it cannot be used thereafter for biscuit or conventional glaze. An outdoor kiln for salt glazing can be quite inexpensive to build, though it will only last a few years.

The arrival of the space-age ceramic fibre referred to at the beginning of this chapter, and the equally revolutionary 'Sayvit' light-weight insulation bricks from America, have reduced the amount of insulation needed for a kiln to work properly. The weight and size of the structural elements having been reduced, the structure itself can be modified and simplified, just as a modern cathedral would no longer be designed to have a stone vault. Light-weight bricks which take up heat and ceramic fibres, pressed into thin sheets like plaster-board, can form the fabric of a kiln with a chamber size of five or six cubic feet—a useful size for the studio potter—whilst weighing only about 100 kilos. A kiln like this can be fitted in an upstairs room, provided there is adequate ventilation and protection against fire.

Electric kilns with elements bedded in metal sleeves are now available, circular or octagonal in plan, ingeniously designed so that the chamber size can be increased or reduced by inserting or removing insulated rings, much as the volume inside a stack of rubber tyres can be changed by changing the number of tyres.

The flexibility which this gives is advantageous, and even more so is the economy in the use of energy achieved by the high speed at which the light-weight kiln heats up. A kiln can reach a temperature of 1300°C in only five hours, and while this is not appropriate for biscuit firing it saves much fuel for glost firings. Light-weight kilns are also inclined to cool very quickly, and traditionally this has been regarded as somewhat inharmonious to the ceramic process and damaging to the glaze. It seems, however, that the mystique of slow cooling has developed as much because the older generation of kilns *would* only cool slowly, rather than because slow cooling improved the pots.

19 The home potter

Pottery can definitely *not* be made in the kitchen. An individual pot can, of course, especially if it is hand built, but once the simple creative act begins to turn into an absorbing spare-time activity, the stresses and strains of mixing clay with everyday household events becomes unbearable. Pots in the making have big demands for space, and even for special atmospheric conditions, and most pottery processes have a constant demand for a water supply. A bathroom, which provides this latter, can sometimes be persuaded to double as a photographic darkroom, but *not* as a pottery for there is rarely enough space to work, no facilities for electric tools and an uncharitable atmosphere which has something to do with the lack of comfort. If you don't believe me, try it and see.

Clay, though not inherently dirty material, is persistent as dust, and leaves an opaque film when washed surfaces like table tops dry. It does not stain carpets or clothes, though a lot of the materials used with it, such as metal oxides, do and the potter knowing this needs a good deal of enthusiasm to overcome inhibitions about creating a mess even if his work is confined to making clay chess men on a tea tray.

The ideal place for a pottery workshop is an outhouse—preferably a ground floor room which has no other full-time function. Flat dwellers, and those whose homes yield no spare rooms, must forget about making pottery at home. Studio space is not difficult to rent, even in dense cities, and the best bet is probably the evening class workroom, where there are usually some facilities and hopefully some space.

This book is no companion, however, if it cannot encourage those with the bare bones of a pottery workshop to use it effectively, and my own enthusiasm helped me in early days to make a pottery out of an old coal cellar, a room in a boot factory and a conservatory shared with a vine. None of these had any form of carpeting, and bare floors, which can be brushed out and occasionally scrubbed, are of the essence.

Funnily enough, pottery studios in new school and college buildings are often designed on the top floors, or in basements, disadvantages which immediately become obvious to their designers when the heavy equipment and raw materials come to be moved in. School kilns rarely weigh less than 10 cwts, and clay is usually ordered by the ton. This, of course, need not worry the student overmuch, for the end products of his efforts are much lighter and easier to move out, but it is worth bearing in mind when choosing a room for a private workshop. Ground floor rooms are ideal and should have large wide doorways (vital for large kilns) and as much light as possible. All fuel-burning kilns need a flue, and normal chimney stacks are often unsuitable for such bursts of energy, so single-storey buildings are the most convenient, when chimneys have to be built. A running water supply is most important, and a disused wash-house begins to emerge as an ideal starting point.

The trouble with such outbuildings is that they tend to be chilly places in winter, and whilst the kiln, when it is on, brings a great deal of comfort as a kind of gratuitous spin-off, a regular form of heating and insulation against frost damage is most important. One-man studio potteries often produce batches of work, all at the same stage, and I remember seeing the sad results when one such potter's entire exhibition production was splintered by overnight frost whilst 'drying'. It is also hard to work well when hands or feet are cold in winter, and equally, in summer, when the ventilation is poor and the kiln has to be fired.

The kiln is the most important piece of equipment. The home potter buying a new or second-hand kiln must take its measurements carefully, and make sure that he can get it into the workshop. All but the smallest electric kilns need an individual switch gear and special wiring from the mains supply. The capital cost of the kiln can be rather daunting, as explained in Chapter 18, but either money or time must be spent in surmounting this initial hurdle, and until one has done so there can be no pottery.

The kiln comes before the wheel, and immediately opens to the potter a vast range of possibilities. The home potter who is tempted first to get himself a wheel soon regrets it, and is faced with the prospect of taking green ware wrapped in cottonwool or news-paper, and often broken on the way, to be unwillingly fired by a friend at a school or at the local brickworks. It is a disenchanting experience, since the potter has no control over the firing, and if the firing is done by the brickworks or earthenware factory, it can be breathtakingly expensive too.

With a kiln installed, a sturdy workbench, clay and running water, the potter has no obstacles and no excuse. Much more energy making the 'place' right often pushes the end products farther into the future, and can even inhibit the potter. The tools for hand-made pottery are simple, and have already been described. Kitchen knives, wooden modelling tools, hacksaw blades and rolling pins can be easily acquired, as can sandpaper, cutting wire or nylon, and clay additives. Kiln furniture, if not supplied with the kiln, must be bought for it cannot easily be made.

Making and applying glazes requires slightly more sophisticated

tools, principal amongst which is the phosphor-bronze lawn or sieve. Such a sieve, of 100 strands per inch mesh and 8 or 10 inch diameter, is an essential, and it is useful to have a coarser and a finer one (80 and 120 mesh) as well. Those with time to go to country sales can still buy scales, metal buckets, pestles and mortars and enamel jugs and bowls quite cheaply, but the amateur potter with less spare time is well advised to buy new rigid polythene equivalents. He will do well, for rigid polythene is the potter's best friend in the workshop. It is easy to clean, and easy to see when it is not clean; compare a bright orange-handled, nylon-bristled scrubbing brush with its natural wood and bristle forebear. Aesthetics apart, plastics win every time. It is a matter of some shame for the potter that when it comes to pouring, the ceramic jug can never match for drip-free performance the moulded plastic jug, with its crisp lip and liquid-repellent surface. This same jug is also vastly more convenient by having a wide top than its enamel equivalent, which is traditionally narrower at the neck than at the base. One jug, a scrubbing brush, two bowls and one bucket with a lid are minimum requirements.

Balances and scales are very important to the potter not only in measuring glaze ingredients but also in weighing clay. Spring balances are to be avoided; not only are they inaccurate, but often the pans are inconveniently small and they are much slower in use than beam balances, with weights on one side and a pan on the other. A good beam balance will be reassuringly accurate for very small quantities—down to $\frac{1}{4}$ oz (7 grams)—whilst a spring balance never will. Kitchen scales and kitchen rolling pins can be used as pottery equipment, but it is wise to get separate ones as some pottery materials are unhealthy, if not toxic.

A full list of all useful tools is tedious reading, and common sense will indicate the need and the solution in most cases. Storage jars made of glass, with well-fitting lids, as described in Chapter 13, are helpful for glazes and dry materials that can absorb moisture (materials which absorb dampness from the atmosphere are not only no longer dry, they are also heavier, and therefore give an inaccurate figure when weighed). Sponges, both synthetic and real, pins, corks and paintbrushes are required and must be kept clean. It is equally important to have a regular place—such as a handy shelf over the wheel—to store the smaller tools like chamois leather strips, as otherwise these can all too easily disappear into the clay waste and the slop bin.

Points to look for in buying second-hand wheels are possible wear in the bearings within which the wheel-head revolves, and in the case of powered wheels the amount of resistance the power source can stand (i.e. pressure on the wheel-head) before the driving mechanism slips. A useful test is this: try to stop the wheel-head when under full power by grasping its sides with both hands. If you can do this easily, then do not buy the wheel. It is a test which should equally be applied to new wheels, for the power provided varies greatly. A problem for the buyer of a new wheel is that the product is not normally on show, and the potter is usually committed to purchase, and to pay carriage, before he can try it.

An electric wheel in a workshop will need a power point, but no special wiring. It should be located in a good light, preferably under a window. If there is drainage for the water tray under the wheel-head, it will probably consist of a short tube or pipe, poised ready to spew clay slip all over the floor. It should not be directed into a drain as the clay content will quickly cause a blockage, and ideally should go into a settling pan (like an old glazed sink) with an overflow leading to a drain. The settled clay can then be cleared out periodically and re-used. If no drainage is available, aim the rubber pipe into as large a vessel as possible and try to remember to empty it before it overflows. Some wheels have a plastic water-catching tray which can be emptied only by removing the wheel-head first, which is sometimes hard work.

Every pottery I have ever known has suffered from a lack of shelf space. Ware drying, awaiting glazing, finishing or firing, and completed work on display all need a place. Working surfaces must be kept clear, and batteries of adjustable shelves are most useful. The discovery that the only unfilled shelf is too low to accommodate a freshly-made pot comes just as one is about to slide the pot on to it, and clearing suitable spaces before making a batch of pots repays the effort involved. Shelves consisting of loose planks of wood resting on dowels between uprights (like ladders with rungs) are the most easy to adjust.

A pottery studio at home may be in use every day, but even if it is not, a fairly frequent check on the state of freshly thrown pots can be made, and the need for a damp-atmosphere cupboard is less vital than at the evening class, attended once weekly. The home potter can nevertheless be caught out by green-ware drying out overnight, especially if the kiln is in use, and a fairly airtight cupboard is a useful asset. If a so-called 'damp' cupboard is made of wood it will warp, and if it is metal it will certainly rust, so it is best to use something which is old and valueless. Polythene bags can be used to maintain a damp atmosphere around coil and slab pots in the making, but they cannot be used on wet thrown ware which shows the mark of anything which touches it. The best way of preserving the dampness of a freshly thrown pot is to invert another pot or tin over it, and to seal the junction with the shelf by means of a ring of clay. Such extreme measures, however, are rarely necessary in a workshop when it is in regular use, and it is good for both pots and pottery room to keep projects alive and progressing.

Some work, like the drying of tiles, cannot be hurried and takes up space. So, of course, do glaze tests, glass jars, clay for re-use and kiln shelves and furniture. Successful pots soon disappear from the workshop but failures and near-failures linger. To have imperfect and stodgy work around has a very depressing effect, and the potter should make a determined effort, and throw it away.

20 Self-help

I have an aunt who, with more affection than discrimination, has kept an embarrassing record of my early progress through the hazards of learning to be a potter. More depressing than a photographic album of one's childhood is to see arranged, but tactfully rarely in use, heavy tableware unsuitably glazed, experimental pottery, first attempts at wax resist and slip trailing, or composite structures so badly balanced that a quick sudden breath should send them toppling but, alas, never has.

The sight of these all-too-permanent reminders of skills hard learned recalls the ultimate ignominy of once, having decided to consign an ugly pot to oblivion, being quite unable to break it against the metal side of a dustbin because of the very thickness of its walls. Unlike early mistakes of an architect which loom large in the city to the general inconvenience of everyone, poor pottery, unless it gets into the hands of my aunt, has a short life. The heavy uncomfortable jug, the impractical and scratchy vase, the dull-ringing stoneware bowl, all these witnesses to bad design and execution undermine one's pride in one's work, and can be banished. Conversely, the senses collectively quicken to the beautiful pot. Dissatisfaction with the quality of one's work in ceramics is a route not to despair but to fulfilment, since a hand-made pot can always be better next time, and the amateur potter can devote time to making it so.

Results in pottery reflect people's moods, and it sometimes seems that one's work, especially on the wheel, is going to pieces rather than improving. Even expert throwers have 'off-days', when it is better not to work on the wheel but to choose another technique. There are so many styles and types of ceramics that one is never at a loss for something to do.

As a teacher, I am always delighted to find a variety of intentions and abilities amongst people who are taking up pottery for the first time. My heart sinks a little, it is true, when someone makes it clear that their main objective in starting is to provide Christmas presents for all their friends and relations (a nearly impossible task anyway if the course only begins in September), but beginners respond quickly to one technique or another, and variety of work and interests is good for morale. If the beginner wants to make tableware, decorated bowls, flower vases, sculptural forms with no useful purpose, or painted tile panels, there is nothing to stop him. Pottery is totally self-justifying and can delight because of its well-designed practical qualities, or simply because it is beautiful.

Traditional jars, contemporary.

Working in clay quickly makes people more responsive to pottery in general, more critical of manufactured ware and more interested in museum collections and contemporary galleries. A regular but short weekly lesson whets the appetite, and beginners in pottery can help themselves by seeking the stimulus of exhibitions, where other people's work and standards can revolutionise their whole approach to the subject. The expressive emotional use of clay in modern sculptural ceramics sometimes sends visitors reeling with shock from galleries, or simply angry because of the way in which ceramic artists of today react against the traditions of the past. The imagination has always worked its way with clay, and five or six thousand years of experiment, tradition and reaction have brought no conclusion other than the certain continuity of the art form. The shaping of a small open bowl from clay is as basic now—and as full of potential—as it was in the time of Mycenae, Akhenaten or Atahualpa. The problem is that today's bowl is unlikely to be as good.

Suppliers of materials are listed on pages 161–4. Many of these sources of equipment produce catalogues which are well illustrated and extremely informative. Many books are available to help the potter, some of which have already been mentioned in earlier chapters, but outstanding is *A Potter's Book* by Bernard Leach which conveys beautifully the excitement and satisfaction of pottery as a hobby or as a way of life.

As a regular and up-to-date lifeline of information, *Ceramic Review*, published by the Craftsmen Potters Association of Great Britain, at 17a Newburgh Street, London W.1., is much appreciated by professional and amateur potters, giving helpful information, serious criticism, and excellent value. In America, *Craft Horizons*, published bimonthly from 44 West 53rd Street, New York, deals with all creative crafts, but ceramics get the lion's share. Both magazines give details of courses, or regular lessons. Full-time training is available in many art schools and craft centres.

There are hundreds of ceramics studios and cooperatives in the United States and in Britain, and it is not difficult to make contact with the potters who run them. The American Crafts Council, 44 West 53rd Street, New York, N.Y. 10019, serves as a clearing house for information about organisations of potters. It is not necessary, of course, to belong to an association or a group of any sort in order to progress in making pottery, though it does seem that a polarisation of views is inevitable—the usual opposition of forces which produces good art—emphasising either the functionalism and good design of a medium which started and continues to serve the table, or the aesthetic and emotional potential of the medium—clay—as a means of communication. It is only this schism of views which is artificial, and good pots will continue to communicate their quality and beauty when the talking is over and done.

Suppliers

All the following suppliers provide catalogues free on request or at the price specified. Except where noted they carry a full range of materials and equipment.

United States of America

A. D. ALPINE (kilns, wheels), 353 Coral Circle, El Segundo, Calif. 90245.

AKG & COMPANY INC., 1442 Christiana Road, Newark, Del. 19711. (302) 738-6590. Catalogue $.35.

AMACO (American Art Clay Company), 4717 West 16th Street, Indianapolis, Ind. 46222. (317) 244-6871.

AMHERST POTTERS SUPPLY, 44 McClellan Street, Amherst, Mass. 01002. (413) 253-9360.

A.R.T. STUDIO, 2725 West Howard Street, Chicago, Ill. 60645. (312) 465-3288. Catalogue $1.00.

BERGEN ARTS & CRAFTS, P.O. Box 381, Marblehead, Mass. 01945.

DICK BLICK COMPANY, P.O. Box 1267, Galesburg, Ill. 61401. (309) 343-6181.

BOIN ARTS & CRAFTS, 87 Morris Street, Morristown, N.J. 07960. (201) 539-0600. Catalogue $.50.

BONA VENTURE SUPPLY COMPANY, 17 Village Square, Hazelwood, Mo. 63042. (314) 895-1008. Catalogue $1.00.

ARTHUR BROWN & BRO INC. (clays, tools, wheels), 2 West 46th Street, New York, N.Y. 10036. (212) 575-5555.

BYRNE CERAMICS SUPPLY COMPANY INC., 95 Bartley Road, Flanders, N.J. 07836. (201) 584-7492.

CLAY ART CENTER (kilns, wheels), 40 Beech Street, Port Chester, N.Y. 10573. (914) 937-2047, 939-9508. 342 Western Avenue, Brighton, Mass. (617) 787-3612.

COLE CERAMIC LABORATORIES, Northeastern Ofc., Box 248, Sharon, Conn. 06069. (203) 364-5025.

THE CRAFTERS INC., P.O. Box 136, Cascade, Wisc. 53011. Catalogue $.50.

THE CRAFTOOL COMPANY INC. (kilns, tools, wheels), 1421 West 240th Street, Harbor City, Calif. 90710. (213) 325-9696. Catalogue $1.00 (free to schools and institutions when requested on official letterhead).

CREEK–TURN CERAMIC SUPPLY, Rte. 38, Hainesport, N.J. 08036. (609) 267-1170. Catalogue $1.00.

CROSS CREEK CERAMICS INC. (clays, glazes, tools), 3596 Brownsville Road, Pittsburgh, Pa. 15227. (412) 881-5425.

DENVER FIRE CLAY CO., P.O. Box 5507, Denver, Co. 80217

EARTHWORKS INC., 2309 West Main Street, Richmond, Va. 23220. (804) 358-8810.

FERRO CORPORATION, 4150 East 56th Street, Cleveland, Ohio 44150.

THE FORMING COMPANY–CERAMIC SUPPLIES, 2764 N.W. Thurman Street, Portland, Ore. 97210. (503) 222-1530.

J. L. HAMMETT COMPANY, 10 Hammett Place, Braintree, Mass. 02184. (617) 848-1000.

HOUSE OF CERAMICS INC., 1011 North Hollywood Street, Memphis, Tenn. 38108. (901) 324-3851. Catalogue $1.00.

KENTUCKY-TENNESSEE CLAY CO., Box 447, Mayfield, Ky 42066.

KILNS SUPPLY & SERVICE CORP., 38 Bulkley Avenue, Port Chester, N.Y. 10573. (914) 937-0007. Catalogue $.60.

LESLIE CERAMIC SUPPLY COMPANY, 1212 San Pablo Avenue, Berkeley, Calif. 94706. (415) 524-7363.

MACMILLAN ARTS & CRAFTS INC., 9520 Baltimore Avenue, College Park, Md. 20740. (301) 441-2420.

MARIN CERAMIC SUPPLY INC., 23 Simms Street, San Rafael, Calif. 94901. (415) 456-7330.

MARSHALL CRAFT (clays, tools, wheels), 1001 Martin Avenue, Santa Clara, Calif. 95050. (408) 248-5544.

MILLER CERAMICS, 8934 North Seneca Street, Weedsport, N.Y. 13166. (315) 689-6253.

MINNESOTA CLAY COMPANY, 8001 Grand Avenue S., Bloomington, Minn. 55420. (612) 884-9101. Catalogue $1.00.

NASCO ARTS & CRAFTS, 901 Janesville Avenue, Fort Atkinson, Wisc. 53538. (414) 563-2446. 1524 Princeton Avenue, Modesto, Calif. 95352. (209) 529-6957.

NEWTON POTTERS SUPPLY INC., 96 Rumford Avenue, P.O. Box 96, West Newton, Mass. 02165. (617) 893-1200.

OHIO CERAMIC SUPPLY INC., P.O. Box 630, 2681 State Rte. 59, Kent, O. 44240. (216) 296-3815. Catalogue $1.00.

PARAMOUNT CERAMICS INC., 220 North State Street, Fairmont, Minn. 56031. (507) 235-3461. Catalogue $1.00.

THE POTTERY SUPPLY HOUSE, P.O. Box 192, 2070 Speers Road, Oakville, Ont. L6J 5A2, Canada. (416) 827-1129.

THE POVERTY BAY POTTERY & CLAY COMPANY (clays, glazes, tools, wheels), 3327 Meridian N., Seattle, Wash. (206) 632-2616.

ROVIN CERAMICS, 6912 Schaefer Road, Dearborn, Mich. 48126. (313) 581-4400. Catalogue $.50.

SACRAMENTO CERAMICS & POTTERS SUPPLY, 2552-C Albatross Way, Sacramento, Calif. 95815. (916) 925-7194. Catalogue $1.00.

SAX ARTS & CRAFTS, 316 N. Milwaukee Street, P.O. Box 2002, Milwaukee, Wisc. 53201. (414) 272-4900. Catalogue $1.00.

SCARGO POTTERY, Dennis, Cape Cod, Mass.

SCULPTURE HOUSE, 38 East 30th Street, New York, N.Y. 10016. (212) 679-7474. Catalogue $1.00.

SHEFFIELD POTTERY INC. (glazes, wheels), Box 395 Rte. 7, Sheffield, Mass. 01257. (413) 229-7700.

STEWART CLAY COMPANY, 133 Mulberry Street, New York, N.Y. 10013. (212) 226-7454.

STEWART'S OF CALIFORNIA INC., 16055 Heron Avenue, La Mirada, Calif. 90638. (714) 523-2603.

TEPPING STUDIO SUPPLY COMPANY, 3003 Salem Avenue, Dayton, O. 45406. (513) 274-1114. Catalogue $1.00.

TRIARCO INC. (kilns, tools, wheels), 7330 North Clark Street, Chicago, Ill. 60626. (312) 338-7220. (Outlets in Fla., Mich., Minn., Pa., Tex., Va.) Catalogue $1.00.

UNITED CLAY MINES CORPORATION, 101 Oakland Street, Trenton, NJ. 08606.

VAN HOWE CERAMIC SUPPLY COMPANY, 11975 East 40th Avenue, Denver, Colo. 80239. (303) 371-4030. Catalogue $1.25.

WAY-CRAFT, 394 Delaware South, Imperial Beach, Calif. 92032. (714) 424-3250.

WESTERN CERAMICS SUPPLY COMPANY, 1601 Howard Street, San Francisco, Calif. 94103. (415) 861-7019. Catalogue $1.00 (free to schools and institutions when requested on official letterhead).

JACK D. WOLFE COMPANY INC., 724 Meeker Avenue, Brooklyn, N.Y. 11222. (212) EV=7-3604. Catalogue $1.00.

Britain

CROMARTIE KILNS (kilns), Park Hall Road, Longton, Staffs.

F. S. DEXTER (kiln plans), Council for Small Industries in Rural Areas, 35 Camp Road, Wimbledon Common, London S.W.19.

FIREGAS KILNS LTD (kilns), Sneyd Street, Stoke-on-Trent, Staffs.

FORDHAM THERMAL SYSTEMS CO. LTD (Sayvit Holden Kiln Kit), 37 Mildenhall Road, Fordham, Ely, Cambs

THE FULHAM POTTERY CO., 210 New King's Road, London S.W.6.

HARRISON MEYER LTD, Craft and Education Division, Meir, Stoke-on-Trent, Staffs.

KASENIT LTD (kilns), Denbeigh Road, Bletchley, Bucks.

KILNS AND FURNACES LTD (kilns), Keele Street Works, Tunstall, Stoke-on-Trent, Staffs.

LASER KILNS (kilns), 38 Seymour Buildings, Seymour Place, London W1

MIDLAND MONOLITHIC FURNACE LINING CO. LTD (kilns), Barnwell, Leicester

MILLS AND HUBBALL LTD (kilns), Victoria Rise, Clapham Common, London S.W.4.

MOIRA POTTERY CO. LTD (clays), Moira, Leicestershire

MORGAN REFRACTORIES ('T' material clay), Neston, Wirral, Cheshire

PODMORE & SONS LTD, Shelton, Stoke-on-Trent, Staffs.

POTCLAYS LTD (general supplies and Amaco lightweight kilns), Brickkiln Lane, Etruria, Stoke on Trent, Staffs.

POTTERS EQUIPMENT CO. LTD (wheels), 17–18 Progress Way, Croydon, Surrey

J. W. RATCLIFF & SONS (wheels), Rope Street, Shelton New Road, Stoke-on-Trent, Staffs.

WATTS, BLAKE, BEARNE & CO. LTD (clays), Courtenay Park, Newton Abbot, Devon

WENGERS LTD (general suppliers, including Fibakilns), Etruria, Stoke on Trent, Staffs.

Australia & New Zealand

RUSSELL COWAN PTY, LTD., 128–138 Pacific Highway, Waitara, N.S.W. 2077.

POTTERY SUPPLIES, 51 Castlemaine Street, Milton, Queensland 4064.

WALKER CERAMICS, Boronia Road, Wantirna, Victoria 3152.

THE CAMDEN ART SUPPLIES, 67 York Street, Launceston, Tasmania 7250

THE PUG MILL, 17A Rose Street, Mile End, S. Australia 5031.

JACKSONS CERAMIC SUPPLIES, 391 Hay Street, Subiaco W. Australia 6008.

TOWNSVILLE ART & FRAMING, 671 Flinders Street, Townsville, Queensland 4810.

HUNTER VALLEY ART SUPPLIES, 31–33 Lambton Road, Broadmeadow, N.S.W. 2292.

C.C.G. INDUSTRIES LTD., 33 Crowhursts Street, New Market, Auckland 1

Glossary

Definitions of most of the raw materials used in making clays and glazes are given in Chapter 12, from pages 100 to 105.

Banding wheel or 'whirler' A freely revolving metal wheel-head mounted on a pedestal base, the latter ranging from a few inches to several feet in height. There is no mechanical means of rotating the wheel-head; it is turned by hand and is used to help in the decoration of the pot (see Chapter 17) or simply to turn the pot around.

Bat A flat portable working surface. Circular bats made from wood, metal, asbestos, plaster or fired clay are useful surfaces on which to make or store pots. Kiln shelves are also sometimes called bats.

Batwash A mixture of flint and water, painted thinly on to kiln shelves which have become spotted with glaze droppings to prevent the sticking of ware.

Biscuit Pottery which has been fired to an insoluble but porous state, like a plant-pot.

Body The clay which forms the structure or fabric of a pot.

Celadon Stoneware glazes containing iron which produce green, grey and grey-blue colours in reduction firing.

Chuck A hollow form, usually expendable and made of plastic clay, but sometimes permanent and made of plaster or metal, which will grip a pot on a wheel-head for stability during the turning process.

Coiled pottery Hand-made pottery in which rolls of clay are built one upon another in rings, or in a continuous spiral, to make a hollow shape.

Composite pots Ware which is the result of assembling separate units, possibly made by different techniques. Thus a composite candelabra may have a slab plinth, a coiled stem and thrown candle-holders.

Crazing The cracking of glaze on the surface of pottery caused by greater contraction in the glaze than in the body of the pot during cooling.

Deflocculant A substance which, acting chemically on plastic clay, gives it liquid characteristics with the addition of very little water. Sodium silicate and sodium carbonate work this magic.

Earthenware Glazed pottery fired to a temperature of 1,000–1,100°C and in which the body remains unvitrified.

Fettling Tidying up or trimming a pot in preparation for firing. The term is most commonly used in industry for the stage in which mould seams are shaved off green pots.

Flux A melting agent which causes silica to form glaze or glass.

Foot ring The circlet of clay at the base of certain thrown pieces which raises the form from the surface on which it stands, and is shaped and hollowed during the turning stage.

Frit A glaze material consisting of flux and silica melted together and reground to a fine powder.

Glost Glaze or glazed. Thus a glost firing is the firing of glazed ware.

Green Unfired pots are described as 'green' or 'green ware' when they are dry and awaiting their first firing.

Grog Ground-down fired pottery, varying in coarseness from the texture of granulated sugar to that of flour, added to plastic clay to quicken drying, add texture or decrease shrinkage.

Kidney A kidney-shaped tool made of flexible steel for finishing pots thrown on a wheel, or made of stiff rubber for pressing and smoothing clay in a mould.

Leather-hard or cheese-hard An important stage in the progress of a pot from raw clay to finished ware. A leather-hard pot is dry enough not to stick to your fingers, but will be soft enough to allow some working of its shape without cracking or other damage.

Lawn A sieve with fine mesh made from phosphor-bronze.

Majolica Earthenware glazed with opaque tin glaze and painted with oxides. Known in Italy as majolica (from Majorca), in France as faience (from Faenza), in England as Delft-ware (from Delft), its true origin is probably North African or Persian.

Maturing temperature The temperature at which a glaze exhibits its best qualities. A variation of $10^{\circ}C$ on either side of the optimum or maturing temperature is enough to spoil the result.

Muffle The refractory chamber inside a fuel-burning kiln which contains the pottery and protects it from the flames.

Oxidised Fired with an adequate supply of oxygen, so that combustion is complete and oxides show bright colours.

Plastic When applied to clay plastic means capable of being shaped and of retaining its shape.

Porcelain White stoneware, usually translucent, made from clay prepared from feldspar, china clay, flint and whiting. Also known imprecisely as 'china'.

Press mould Strictly speaking, a press mould is a two-piece plaster mould which, when assembled, squeezes plastic clay like ham in a sandwich into a precise profile. It is often used to describe a single mould into which plastic clay is pressed by hand or with a tool.

Raw Raw clay is unfired clay and raw glazing is the technique of applying a glaze to an unfired pot, and heating both clay and glaze up together. The resulting ware is often called once-fired ware.

Reduced Fired in an oxygen-starved atmosphere (either by restricting the inflow of air or introducing a substance which combines with oxygen in burning). Reduction firing relates to stoneware and the effect is to reduce the colour of metal oxides to the colour of the metals themselves.

Saggar A protective fireclay box, usually round in section, for holding pottery in fuel-burning kilns without muffles.

Seger cone A pyroscope named after its inventor and designed to indicate heat work by melting. Seger cones are not cones but small slender pyramids of fusible material like glaze which bend over as a precise temperature is reached.

Slab pottery Hand-built pottery made by assembling flat slabs of clay.

Slip Clay in a very liquid state, used in casting (see Chapter 11) and in decoration (see Chapter 16).

Stoneware Glazed pottery in which both body and glaze are fused together in a non-porous vitrified state, as a result of firing to temperatures above 1,200°C.

Throwing The technique of making pots with the hands from plastic clay on a wheel.

Turning The technique of trimming thrown pots using metal and other tools when the pots have become leather hard.

Wedging The cutting and re-forming of lumps of plastic clay preparatory to kneading to ensure an even texture.

Wheel-head The circular flat disc attached to the revolving spindle of a potter's wheel, and on which the pot is formed.

Picture Credits

The author would like to thank the following for kindly supplying and granting permission to use photographs: Maggie Berkowitz, British Museum, Alan Caiger-Smith, Derek Clarkson, *Ceramic Review*, Crafts Advisory Council, *Crafts Magazine*, English China Clays, Jane Hamlyn, Michael Holford, Peter Kinnear, Eric Mellon, Kevan Pegley, Jacqui Poncelet, James Tower, Victoria and Albert Museum, Eric Webster. All other photographs copyright Alphabet and Image.

Index